Bedtime

A FAMILY COMPANION

Special thanks

Ruth Higham wins the Golden Hotwater Bottle for her research and
unflagging support. My husband Tribble has been a guardian angel. Teddies go
to our sons William, Charlie, and Henry for letting me stay up late to work.

An Hachette Livre Company
First published in Great Britain in 2004 by MQ Publications,
a division of Octopus Publishing Group Ltd
2–4 Heron Quays, London E14 4JP
www.octopusbooks.co.uk

ISBN: 978-1-84072-732-6

10 9 8 7 6 5 4 3 2

Printed and bound in China

Bedtime

A FAMILY COMPANION

JANE FURNIVAL

MQP

Contents

7 Introduction • **8** The Bed Timeline • **10** Getting to Sleep • **12** Scented Night Baths • **14** Sleeping Comfortably? • **16** *Pleasant Dreams* • **18** Calming Chamomile • **20** *Rip Van Winkle* • **24** Sleep in a Cup • **26** How Are You Sleeping? • **28** Don't Lose Sleep Over It, But… • **30** Feng Shui for Bedrooms • **32** A Romantic Haven • **34** Sweet Sleep • **36** Make a Herbal Sleep Pillow • **42** Early Beds • **44** Bed Warmers • **46** Hot Water Bottles • **48** Bed Genius • **50** *It's Raining, It's Pouring* • **52** Healthy Habits • **54** Caring for Fine Linens • **56** Buying Bed Linen • **58** Recipes for Tired Bed Linen • **60** Scenting the Bed Linen • **64** The Well-Made Bed • **68** Hot Foot • **70** A Much-Loved Bedside Nurse • **72** The Lady of the Lamp • **74** *The Casualty Clearing Station* • **76** *Sense and Sensibility* • **84** Sleep-Talking • **86** Snoring • **88** *Wee Willie Winkie* • **90** Baby's Room • **94** The Lullaby • **96** Brahms' Lullaby • **104** Lovable Bed Companions • **108** Make a Teddy Bear • **114** Moses Baskets • **116** *Fais Dodo* • **118** Food for Happy Dreams • **120** *There Was an Old Person of Rheims* • **122** Bedroom Cocktails • **124** Grandes Horizontales • **126** Bedroom Farce • **130** The Bedroom Slipper • **132** A Bedtime Indulgence • **134** Nightcaps • **136** Silk and Satin Sheets • **137** Dressed for the Night • **140** Pajamas • **142** Following the Equator • **144** Personalize Your Slippers • **146** Bedtime Beauty Routines • **148** Beauty Before Bed • **150** The Celestial Bed • **152**

Dreams • **154** *Dreams* • **156** Dream Interpretation • **162** Make a Dream Journal • **164** Nightmares • **166** *Sleeping Beauty* • **170** Guardian Angels • **172** Children's Dream Beds • **174** Hammocks As Beds • **176** Make a Hammock • **180** *The Beautiful Land of Nod* • **182** *Heidi* • **184** Slumber Parties • **188** Make a Sleepy Bear Pajama Case • **194** The Tooth Fairy • **196** Make an Apple Pie Bed • **198** Beds in the Middle Ages • **200** Bed Superstitions • **202** Bed Sizes • **204** *Goldilocks and the Three Bears* • **206** Bed Testing • **210** Finding the Right Bed • **214** *Snow White* • **216** The Well-Tempered Mattress • **218** *The Princess and the Pea* • **220** Inner Springs • **222** Don't Let the Bedbugs Bite! • **224** In My Lady's Chamber • **226** Canopy Beds • **230** *Weaves And Draperies, Classic and Modern* • **234** Wallbeds • **236** Japanese Sleeping Capsules • **238** Power Napping • **240** Pillow Talk • **244** The Pillow Book • **248** Pillow and Duvet Fillings • **250** Alarm Clocks • **254** The Sunne Rising • **256** The Automatic Tea-Maker • **258** Up With the Rooster? • **260** Elsie Marley • **262** Breakfast in Bed • **266** Braveheart's Breakfast • **268** Bedtime Prayer • **270** *The House of Mirth* • **274** Guest Bedrooms • **276** An American Original • **280** The Rise of Twin Beds • **282** Make a Quilt • **290** American Trade Blankets • **292** Wedding Nights • **294** The Great Bed of Ware • **296** Bed Racing • **300** Iron Beds • **301** Ghosties and Ghoulies • **304** Picture Credits

Introduction

What bliss—it's time for bed! Time to slow down, forget all the hustle and bustle of your busy day, pull back the bedcovers, and curl up with *Bedtime: A Family Companion*. And what delightful pleasures await you between these covers; here you are sweetly welcomed into the cozy world of bed.

This cleverly composed bedtime "bible" creates a unique sleepytime world. Bedtime is its very own kingdom—a fascinating, curious place composed of quirky facts, stories, myths, lullabies, and quotations from poetry and literature from around the world. You'll be visually enchanted too—each page reveals one amusing, amazing delight after another in an eclectic mix of dreamy and evocative illustrations and photographs.

Bedtime: A Family Companion embraces everyone, young or old. We took our first steps into the Land of Nod Sleep listening to lullabies, fairy tales, and nursery rhymes—and these still charm and enchant children and grownups today. Meanwhile, classic stories, famous musings, and quotations taken from history and literature will give you time to wonder and reflect, long after young folk have gone to sleep.

There's plenty to satisfy the curious mind and practical hand, also. Find out who slept in which bed, how to keep sheets fresh and crisp, how to make a patchwork quilt, cure insomnia, buy a mattress, and make bedtime drinks. Discover how the Egyptians slept, and explore every aspect of bedtime, including dreamlore, nightwear, bed companions, pillows, sheets, angels, and bed covers.

Bedtime: A Family Companion is a book of timeless treasure, an illluminating and evocative portrait of the beautiful, alluring, mysterious world of sleep and all its rituals and paraphernalia. Keep it at your bedside as a perfect companion, to enjoy on your own, and with your loved ones.

The Bed Timeline

ANCIENT EGYPT

The Egyptians use couches for eating and sleeping on. Advanced beds are made of wood veneered with ivory or ebony, and given finely carved legs. Hard headrests, not pillows, are used to support the head.

ANCIENT GREECE & ROMAN EMPIRE

The Greeks and Romans also recline on couches and develop truly

luxurious beds. They are frequently piled high with covers, rugs, and animal skins, and decorated with gold or silver.

MIDDLE AGES

The lower classes sleep on pallet beds or benches while the wealthy rest on heavy wooden, often canopied, beds and feather mattresses.

16TH & 17TH CENTURIES

The expression "sleep tight" comes from the traditional 17th-century beds, which were made of interwoven ropes needing regular tightening. Grand canopy

1865
The first coil-spring construction for bedding is patented.

1900s
Innerspring mattresses and upholstered bed bases gain in popularity. Futons are introduced to North America. In the 1960s, the waterbed appears on the bed scene, followed by airbeds.

beds come into fashion, decked with lavish drapes to protect against drafts and to maintain privacy.

19TH CENTURY
Iron and brass bedsteads replace traditional wood and become commonplace in many homes.

9

Getting to Sleep

We sleep an average of two hours less than our grandparents. Yet two in ten people suffer from insomnia and only 55 percent of men and 37 percent of women say they sleep well. If you are "TATT"—medical shorthand for "tired all the time"—you could have low ferritin levels. See the doctor and rule out medical causes.

Do a bedroom audit. Deal with disturbances, like your partner snoring, or too much light. Remove that TV or desk tempting you to stay up. Is your room secure? Too hot, cold, or stuffy?

Are you on a caffeine or alcohol high? Too full or hungry? Limit yourself to one unit of alcohol two hours before sleeping and drink the same in water. Delay bedtime for two hours after eating.

Are you overexcited by exercise before bed, or clubbing? People who do well in life tend to keep regular hours and go home at night.

Give yourself permission to rest. Sleep is not a non-activity, a cop out for when you physically flop. Wind down with a calming film or a bath.

Read a complex book. Try to remember the order of presidents of the United States, recite multiplication, or play music or spoken tapes.

Don't argue before bed or brood on daytime problems. Confide in someone or write it down in a "pillow book" before sleeping, but don't send emotional letters.

If you have had an accident or loss, give yourself several months, minimum, to let your brain recover your sleep patterns.

Find a low-stress hobby before sleeping, like embroidery. Throwing yourself into some new project may help.

If you sometimes think, "What's the point of getting up?" exercise more to raise your serotonin (happiness-releasing chemical). If it doesn't work, see your doctor.

Finally, the golden rule of "sleep hygiene." Bedrooms are sacred to sleep. If you can't sleep, get up and do something—in another room.

Scented Night Baths

Perfect for insomniacs, a warm bedtime bath soothes the senses, eases muscular tension, and has a sedative effect on the mind. Try using night-perfumed plants like honeysuckle or sweet rocket. Then, when you want a super-scented bath at night, pick the petals freshly. Put them into a muslin bag, tie with ribbon and swoosh through the warm bath water. Do not sprinkle petals onto the bath, or you might lose sleep calling a plumber to unclog your drains. Make sure you can emerge from the bath directly into freshly laundered sheets (in winter pop a hot water bottle between the sheets before running the bath.)

THE PERFECT BEDTIME BATH

Caution: omit marjoram oil during pregnancy and chamomile and lavender in the first trimester.

Ingredients

- **3 drops essential oil of chamomile**
- **3 drops essential oil of marjoram**
- **2 drops essential oil of lavender**

1 Run a very warm, deep bath. Just before stepping in, drop the essential oils into the water and swish to disperse.

2 Relax for 20 minutes or more with a calming book.

3 When you feel your eyes closing, pat yourself dry and head for bed. Before you hit the pillow, place two drops of lavender oil on the edge of the pillowcase. Alternatively, apply the oil to a tissue and place on the pillow or put three drops of frankincense and one of myrrh essential oil onto your cold bedside light, to evaporate subtly as the bulb warms.

Bedtime for Babies

To help soothe babies before bed, bathe them in the early evening, heating two drops of essential oil of lavender in water in an oil vaporizer to scent the room. Follow with a calming massage using a little sweet almond oil. Spritz the nursery with two drops of lavender oil in water in an atomizer.

Sleeping Comfortably?

If you want an insight into somebody's true personality, simply look at the way he or she sleeps. Scientists believe the position in which a person goes to sleep provides an important clue about his or her character. Professor Chris Idzikowski, director of the Sleep Assessment and Advisory Service in the UK, has analyzed six common sleeping positions—and found that each is linked to a particular personality type.

"We are all aware of our body language when we are awake but this is the first time we have been able to see what our subconscious posture says about us. What's interesting is that the profile behind the posture is often very different from what we would expect."

The Fetus: Those who curl up in the fetus position are described as tough on the outside but sensitive at heart. They may be shy when they first meet somebody, but soon relax. This appears to be the most common sleeping position and is more popular with women than men.

The Soldier: Lying on their back with both arms by their sides, these people are generally quiet and reserved. They don't like a fuss, but set high standards for themselves and others.

The Log: Those who lie on their side with both arms down by their side are easy going, social people who like being part of the in-crowd and who are trusting of strangers. However, they may be gullible.

The Yearner: People who sleep on their side with both arms out in front are said to have an open nature, but can be suspicious and cynical. They are slow to make up their minds, but once they have, they are unlikely ever to change it.

The Freefall: People who lie on their front with their hands around the pillow and their head turned to one side are often gregarious and brash people, but can also be high-strung and thin-skinned underneath. They usually don't like criticism or extreme situations.

The Starfish: Lying on their back with both arms up around the pillow, these sleepers make good friends because they are always ready to listen to others, and offer help when needed. They generally don't like to be the center of attention.

Incidentally, the freefall position is good for digestion, while the starfish and soldier positions are more likely to lead to snoring and a bad night's sleep.

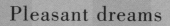

Pleasant dreams

And sweet repose;

If you lie on your back,

You won't hurt your nose.

Calming Chamomile

The pretty white and yellow flowers of the chamomile plant are a wonderful natural remedy, used for centuries to encourage feelings of calm and relaxation and to aid the sleepless. Chamomile can be made into a mild tea for a relaxing and soothing effect on the nervous and digestive systems. Drinking a delicious and aromatic cup of chamomile tea before bed may soothe an anxious mind, as well as treating insomnia. Taking a bath in water infused with chamomile oil will also help you to unwind—especially if you surround your bathtub with chamomile-scented candles. Aromatic pillows lightly scented with chamomile are a widely-available and delightful treat that may help you gently drift off to sleep at the end of a hard day.

CHAMOMILE TEA

Makes 4–5 cups

- 3 tbsp dried chamomile flowers
- 3 cups/750ml water
- 1 tsp honey per cup to sweeten (optional)

1 Place the chamomile flowers into a warmed teapot, and heat the water to boiling point. Pour it over the flowers.

2 Place the lid on the teapot and allow the tea to steep for ten minutes. Pour it through the strainer and sweeten with honey if desired.

Rip Van Winkle

by

WASHINGTON IRVING

[Rip] reiterated his visits to the flagon so often that at length his senses were overpowered, his eyes swam in his head, his head gradually declined, and he fell into a deep sleep.

On waking, he found himself on the green knoll whence he had first seen the old man of the glen…He looked round for his gun, but in place of the clean well-oiled fowling-piece, he found an old firelock lying by him, the barrel incrusted with rust, the lock falling off, and the stock worm-eaten. He now suspected that the grave roysterers of the mountain had put a trick upon him, and, having dosed him with liquor, had robbed him of his gun. Wolf, too, had disappeared, but he might have strayed away after a squirrel or partridge. He whistled after him and shouted his name, but all in vain; the echoes repeated his whistle and shout, but no dog was to be seen…

It was with some difficulty that he found the way to his own house, which he approached with silent awe, expecting every moment to hear the shrill voice of Dame Van Winkle. He found the house gone to decay—the roof fallen in, the windows shattered, and the doors off the hinges. A half-starved dog that looked like Wolf was skulking about it. Rip called him by name, but the cur snarled, showed his teeth, and passed on.

This was an unkind cut indeed—"My very dog," sighed poor Rip, "has forgotten me!"…

He now hurried forth, and hastened to his old resort, the village inn—but it too was gone. A large rickety wooden building stood in its place, with great gaping windows, some of them broken and mended with old hats and petticoats, and over the door was painted, "the Union Hotel, by Jonathan Doolittle."…There was, as usual, a crowd of folk about the door, but none that Rip recollected. The very character of the people seemed changed. There was a busy, bustling, disputatious tone about it, instead of the accustomed phlegm and drowsy tranquillity…The appearance of Rip, with his long grizzled beard, his rusty fowling-piece, his uncouth dress, and an army of women and children at his heels, soon attracted the attention of the tavern politicians. They crowded round him, eyeing him from head to foot with great curiosity…[Rip] inquired, "Where's Nicholas Vedder?"

There was a silence for a little while, when an old man replied, in a thin piping voice, "Nicholas Vedder! why, he is dead and gone these eighteen years! There was a wooden tombstone in the church-yard that used to tell all about him, but that's rotten and gone too."

"Where's Brom Dutcher?"

"Oh, he went off to the army in the beginning of the war; some say he was killed at the storming of Stony Point—others say he was drowned in a squall at the foot of Antony's Nose. I don't know—he never came back again." ☞

☞ "Where's Van Bummel, the schoolmaster?"

"He went off to the wars too, was a great militia general, and is now in congress."

Rip's heart died away at hearing of these sad changes in his home and friends, and finding himself thus alone in the world. Every answer puzzled him too, by treating of such enormous lapses of time, and of matters which he could not understand: war—congress—Stony Point;—he had no courage to ask after any more friends, but cried out in despair, "Does nobody here know Rip Van Winkle?"

"Oh, Rip Van Winkle!" exclaimed two or three, "Oh, to be sure! That's Rip Van Winkle yonder, leaning against the tree."

Rip looked, and beheld a precise counterpart of himself, as he went up the mountain: apparently as lazy, and certainly as ragged. The poor fellow was now completely confounded. He doubted his own identity, and whether he was himself or another man. In the midst of his bewilderment, the man in the cocked hat demanded who he was, and what was his name?

"God knows," exclaimed he, at his wit's end; "I'm not myself—I'm somebody else—that's me yonder—no—that's somebody else got into my shoes—I was myself last night, but I fell asleep on the mountain, and they've changed my gun, and every thing's changed, and I'm changed, and I can't tell what's my name, or who I am!"

…At this critical moment a fresh comely woman pressed through the throng to get a peep at the gray-bearded man. She had a chubby child in her arms, which, frightened at his looks, began to cry. "Hush, Rip," cried she, "hush, you little fool; the old man won't hurt you." The name of the child, the air of the mother, the tone of her voice, all awakened a train of recollections in his mind. "What is your name, my good woman?" asked he.

"Judith Gardenier."

"And your father's name?"

"Ah, poor man, Rip Van Winkle was his name, but it's twenty years since he went away from home with his gun, and never has been heard of since—his dog came home without him; but whether he shot himself, or was carried away by the Indians, nobody can tell. I was then but a little girl."

Rip had but one question more to ask; but he put it with a faltering voice:

"Where's your mother?"

"Oh, she too had died but a short time since; she broke a blood-vessel in a fit of passion at a New-England peddler."

There was a drop of comfort, at least, in this intelligence. The honest man could contain himself no longer. He caught his daughter and her child in his arms. "I am your father!" cried he—"Young Rip Van Winkle once—old Rip Van Winkle now!—Does nobody know poor Rip Van Winkle?"

All stood amazed, until an old woman, tottering out from among the crowd, put her hand to her brow, and peering under it in his face for a moment, exclaimed, "Sure enough! It is Rip Van Winkle—it is himself! Welcome home again, old neighbor— Why, where have you been these twenty long years?"

The
World's
Best
Night-cup

Sleep in a Cup

RICH HOT CHOCOLATE

Makes 2 mugs

- 2½ cups/600ml milk
- 5½oz/150g bittersweet chocolate, cut up
- ⅔ cup/150ml heavy cream
- unsweetened cocoa powder for dusting

1 Heat the milk in a pan to just below boiling. Stir in the chocolate pieces until melted. Pour into mugs.

2 Whip the cream until barely stiff, then float on top of the hot chocolate. Dust with cocoa powder.

How Are You Sleeping? Are You...

Catching some Z's?

Crashing? Getting your beauty sleep?

Dozing off?

Getting some shut-eye?

Going up the wooden hill to Bedfordshire?

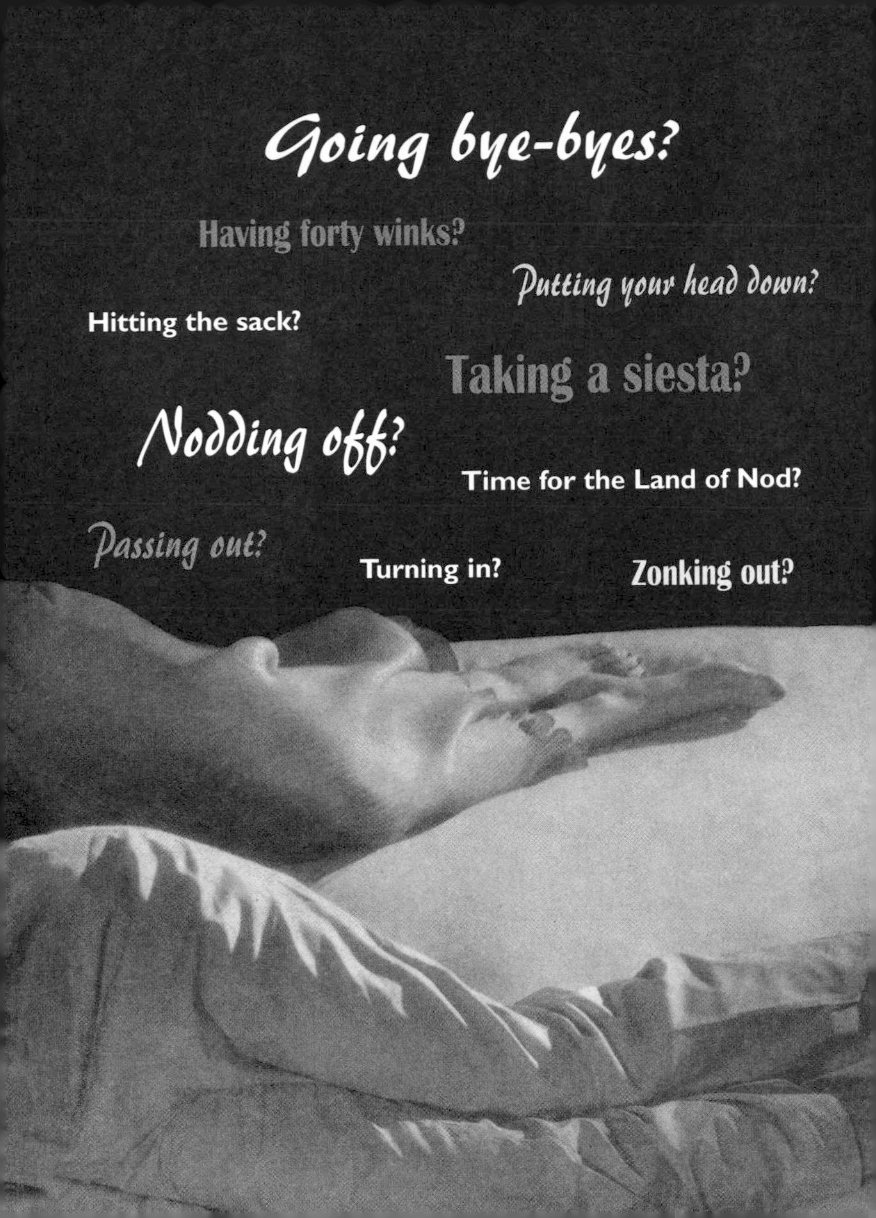
Going bye-byes?
Having forty winks?
Putting your head down?
Hitting the sack?
Taking a siesta?
Nodding off?
Time for the Land of Nod?
Passing out?
Turning in?
Zonking out?

Don't Lose Sleep Over It, But...

- By the time we are 50, we have spent 16 years in bed.

- We perspire as much as $\frac{1}{2}$ pint/250ml each night.

- In a recent survey, five out of ten men complained about their partner's cold feet.

- A bedroom hotter than 75°F/24°C greatly reduces sleep quality.

- Losing an hour's sleep can lower your IQ by one point the next day. But creativity improves up to 20 percent after a good night's sleep.

- While sleeping you burn more calories (85 per hour) than you do watching TV.

- The average adult grows up to two centimeters, or just under an inch each night. Lying down "unwinds" the spine after it has been compressed by standing upright all day.

- A person will die from total lack of sleep sooner than from starvation. Death will occur in about ten days without sleep, while starvation takes a few weeks.

- Sunday is by far the hardest night of the week on which to sleep, according to a recent survey. This problem is probably caused by the prospect of getting up to go to work on Monday. It may also be connected to the disruption of routine, as good sleep is related to regular routine, which can get disrupted on weekends.

Feng Shui for Bedrooms

• Feng shui is the Chinese philosophy of arranging your environment to bring health and happiness.

• Life is a balance between yin, or passive, and yang, or active. Red or yellow bedrooms are yang; blues, greens, or neutral whites are more restful.

• For a strong energy flow, keep your bedroom clean and uncluttered. Avoid water features or seascape paintings, which can presage burglaries. Also try lowering the light wattage.

• To attract romance in your life, feng shui experts advise making space for it in your bedroom. Remove all objects from past relationships. Don't exercise in your bedroom or store your equipment there.

• Avoid harsh lighting and sharp-cornered bedside lamps and lights or ceiling fans right over the bed, which can emit what is known as "poison arrows."

- Create balance and harmony by placing a bedside table on both sides of the bed.

- The Chinese believe that when you sleep, your soul wanders away from your body. Never position mirrors to reflect the bed. It might confuse the soul so that it re-enters the wrong body, causing a zombie-like state in the sleeper. For undisturbed nights, curtain off mirrors.

- Never position the head or foot of the bed in front of the door. This is known as the "coffin position" and brings bad luck.

A Romantic Haven

With their clean, crisp Gustavian interiors, the Swedish are experts at making a simple bed look stunning. The key is using soft, inexpensive fabrics such as cotton prints, muslin, or even mosquito netting to create a fresh, relaxing haven in which to sleep. Drape this over the bed to give a tent-like look, using a staple gun, and a hot glue gun for fixing.

Suspend a half corona (wooden half-circle) from the wall behind the head of the bed. Use this to gather up fabric, which cascades down around the headboard. Screw a hook into the wall on each side of the bed, and tie the fabric back at the sides. Line the inside of the corona, as this is what you see in bed.

You could also fix a circular corona from the ceiling halfway down the bed. Use it to gather fabric that drapes two ways, over the headboard and the headbase. Use an embroidery frame or wire circlet as a corona.

Instead of a corona, minimalists might use a pole, or buy swagholders and attach them to the wall behind the bed. They will secure lengths of fabric without sewing. Try using tassled material or heavy cotton for a decadent feel, or stick to fine, breezy fabrics like muslin to retain that Swedish coolness.

Sweet Sleep

Sachets filled with herbs such as lavender, chamomile, lemon balm, rose petals, and dried hops have been recommended as aids for better sleep for centuries. It is very easy to make your own small sleep pillow filled with your favorite combination of sedative herbs, which can be placed inside the pillowcase. It will release a sweet, calming aroma every time you turn your head in the night. You can also carry your comforting pillow with you when you are traveling and place it between your pillows to remind you of home. In addition to the lavender sleep pillow overleaf, try one of these herbal sleep mixes:

- **For tranquil sleep: 2 tbsp rose petals, woodruff, and lavender, mixed with 1 tsp orris powder to fix the scent**

- **To relax and comfort: 2 tbsp lemon verbena, 1 tbsp dried lavender, and a tsp dried shredded orange peel, a vanilla pod or half a vanilla bean, 1 tsp orris powder**

- **For pleasant dreams: 2 tbsp rose petals and rosemary, 2 tbsp rosemary, 1 tbsp chamomile flowers, 1 tsp orris powder**

"And they shall fetch thee jewels
from the deep And sing, while thou
on pressed flowers dost sleep."

from *A Midsummer Night's Dream*, William Shakespeare

Make a Herbal Sleep Pillow

This beautiful organdy bag, with its classically simple design, can be filled with traditional lavender or any combination of suitable dried herbs to create an attractive and aromatic sachet that will encourage a good night's sleep wherever you are.

MATERIALS
- 12in of 46in-wide organdy
- White silk embroidery thread
- Paper
- Pencil
- Sewing machine
- Sewing kit
- 20in silk cord
- Quilting pencil
- Toggle or button

1 Make a paper template 22 x 9¼in/56 x 25.5cm adding a point at one short end and pin it to the organdy. Fold the organdy in half along the grain and pin the template with the short end on the folded edge keeping the pins within a seam allowance of ½in/1cm. Cut out through both layers of fabric keeping them pinned together.

2 On each long edge, measure 3½in from one end. Mark the point with colored thread in each seam allowance. Machine stitch around the edge of the organdy between the colored threads to form the bag flap. Stitch the other short end. Trim the seam allowance to ⅛in/0.3cm. Clip off the corners and turn through (see figure A).

3 Press the seams flat. Fold the short, straight edge up to meet the start of the flap and press the fold.

4 Pin the side seams and stitch ¼in/0.5cm from the raw edge. Trim the seam allowance to ⅛in/0.3cm and press open as far as possible (see figure B). Turn the bag through and press flat. Stitch

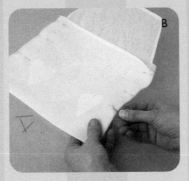

the side seams again
¼in/0.5cm from the edge.
Sew in the thread ends. Turn
the bag through and press.

5 Trace the heart braid-
work template directly
onto the organdy using a
quilting pencil. Fold the cord
in two and pin around the
lines, leaving a small loop to
fasten the bag at the point.

6 Oversew the cord,
stitching through the
top thickness of organdy.
Stitch the loop securely.
Oversew the cord several
times at the end of the
design and snip the cord
close to the stitches (see
figure C).

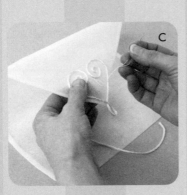

7 Sew a toggle or
button on the bag in
the corresponding position.

"Observation has convinced me that all good and true
book-lovers practise the pleasing and improving
avocation of reading in bed. Indeed, I fully believe with

Judge Methuen that no book can be appreciated until it has been slept with and dreamed over."

from *Love Affairs of a Bibliomaniac*, Eugene Field

Early Beds

Egyptians used the same beds for lounging in the day and sleeping at night. The earliest known models were made of palm sticks or palm-leaf wicker, lashed together with pieces of cord or rawhide. Later, Egyptian bed-makers introduced mortise-and-tenon construction and wood bed frames veneered with ivory or ebony.

More elaborate designs featured rounded poles that were joined together and supported on finely carved legs in the form of animal legs, ranging from heavy bull's legs to gazelle-like forms with hooves, and the feline type with paw and claw, frequently identified as lion's legs.

Many beds sloped down from the headboard. No mattresses have been found, although pictures exist. Instead of pillows, the Egyptians used headrests, made of stone, ivory, or wood. A footboard ensured that the sleeper would not slip off.

The Egyptian Pharaohs embellished their beds with richly carved symbols of animals, fruit, and flowers. These beds were made to last, for eternity, and indeed five beds accompanied King Tutankhamen in his tomb.

Poor Egyptians slept on a mattress filled with straw or wool, or on a mat, or simply the plain floor. Many beds were fitted

with a canopy of some kind from which mosquito netting could be hung. The Greek historian Herodotus claimed that contemporary Egyptians used the nets by day to catch fish.

Shaped like a couches, the beds of the ancient Greeks were used to recline on at meal times and to sleep on at night. The beds were mobile and packed with layers of skins, blankets and rugs, with plenty of pillows and elaborate covers.

The Romans developed the bed as a symbol of wealth and prestige and adapted their designs from the Greeks, with the addition of headboards, footboards, and silk for mattresses and covers. The bed frames were made of wood or finely cast bronze depending on the owner's financial means.

Bed Warmers

Cavemen warmed flat stones in the embers of their cooking fires, then placed them inside beds to take the chill out. Some people do this today, warming a stone in a cool oven then slipping it into a cushion cover to prevent burning.

In seventeenth-century England, this developed into the warming pan, which looked like a long-handled, lidded brass or copper frying pan. It was filled with hot embers from the fire, then moved around under the sheets to warm the bed all over. It was alleged that Queen Anne, wife of James II, smuggled a baby into the royal chamber inside a bed warmer to replace a stillborn child bound for the throne.

By 1830 the Victorians made pretty stoneware bottle "bed warmers" with elaborate names like "The Adaptable Hot Water Bottle and Bed Warmer."

They would crack unless you warmed them before filling them with boiling water. Ensure that the stoppers fit before buying them in antique shops, if you want to use them. They also make great door stoppers.

Hot Water Bottles

There is something sweet and simple about a hot water bottle. You can use it to warm painful parts of your body, and like a pet, it snuggles up to you. Just don't lose it in the bed—finding a cold one next morning is dispiriting. Never overfill a hot water bottle, nor use boiling water, or it will soon break. Remove its cover, to keep it dry, then lie it on its side and gently expel the air as you carefully fill it no more than half full.

Rubber bottles are still made in Germany, and some shops do a roaring trade in mink covers at Christmas. You can also buy "art" designs in thermoplastic. A recent bottle printed with Andy Warhol's Marilyn sold out instantly.

MAKE A PERSONALIZED
HOT WATER BOTTLE COVER

Instructions:

* Use bright-colored felt, folded into double thickness.

* Lay the bottle down and, rather than following the shape closely, trace a rectangle around its outline up to the neck, adding at least 1in/2.5cm around the outside. Cut this out, so you have two fabric shapes. Now is your chance to personalize your bottle cover, sewing on a small soft toy, the user's name, or a collage.

* Then, making sure the bottle will fit inside, sew both sides together in running stitch or blanket stitch on the outside, using a contrasting-color thread. Turn over a tubular hem at the top, leaving the sides of the hem open. Slip a braid through the hem with a hairgrip or darning needle. Pull this braid tight to secure the cover around the bottle.

Bed Genius

There are some gadgets you simply can't sleep without…

If you are prone to overheating when asleep, try Helmer Hedberg's bed-ventilator. This harnesses the power of your breath to lift the bedcovers off your body rhythmically. Some might question why you need a motorized bedcover with pipes sewn into it, when you can just kick the blankets off for a similar effect, but that's science.

Babies need gentler measures, like Thomas Zelenka's 1971 machine to reassure a sleeping infant "by means of periodic pats upon the rump or hind part." This uses a giant motorized hand in a softly padded glove. Just like Mom's!

With Samuel Applegate's "Device for Waking Persons from Sleep," patented in 1882, you never again have to say, "Sorry. I slept through my alarm clock." 60 corks—too light to hurt, surely?—are mounted on a frame above the bed, connected to your alarm clock. When it rings, the corks crash onto your head.

Smoking in bed is dangerous, but for those who can't resist, in 1910, Archie Black unveiled a safety pipe "without danger of igniting the bed clothing." This looked like a hookah. The pipe's stem was a long, flexible hose, leading to the bowl, containing smouldering tobacco, on a bedside table. Mr. Black adds helpfully that during the daytime the bowl can be carried in one's breast pocket.

Some more modern, less outrageous bedtime inventions include: heat and massage options to comfort bad backs and air the bed automatically in the morning, protecting against damp and bed mites; and huge plasma TVs, springing out of the bedbase at the touch of a remote control.

The "Sweat Bed" was invented around 1850
for people suffering from lumbago, rheumatism,
and similar disorders. Unfortunately, the system of
steam pipes under the mattress, which was fed
by a gas-heated generator, had a tendency
to overheat and explode.

It's raining,
   it's pouring;

The old man
   is snoring.

He went to
   bed and he

Bumped
   his head

And he
   couldn't get
   up in the
   morning.

Healthy Habits

- Airing the bed is not an old-fashioned idea. Throw back the bedclothes each morning for twenty minutes—our bodies can shed half a pint of moisture overnight.

- Don't forget the cleansing virtues of fresh air and sunshine. Take your duvets and quilts off the bed, and let them air outdoors for a few hours. They'll soon be sweet-smelling and good as new.

- Never leave plastic wrappings on a mattress, or it will get damp. Washable mattress covers protect mattresses from stains. Allergy-sufferers can get boilable mite-proof covers.

- Use water and a mild washing powder on mattress stains. Dry wet patches with a hairdryer and leave to air as long as possible.

- New mattresses should be turned over sideways and endways every month for the first three months to help them settle.

- Vacuum the bedbase and mattress occasionally to remove dustmites and irritants.

LEFT: *Frau Holle*, by O. Kubel

Caring for Fine Linens

"To look over the linen every Monday morning."

A laundrymaid's duty, laid down in the *Housekeeping Book of Susanna Whatman*, 1776

If you inherit some treasured family linen, it is important to know how to care for and store it. Some affluent households in the 1800s devoted whole rooms to storing fine linen.

Really precious linens should be washed by hand, and it is important that they are thoroughly rinsed as soap residue will spoil the fabric. The linen need not be dried completely—it is easier to iron while damp. However, ironing creases into your linens will cause stress on those areas and possible damage.

Susanna Whatman's linen was probably stored in a linen press, with a huge screw pressing the sheets flat. However, your bedlinen will stay cleaner and fresher if stored on slatted pine shelves, allowing the air to move through them. Screw some hooks close to the edge, and tie bunches of dried scented lavender, geranium leaves, sweet woodruff, or mint for a clean smell that discourages all insects.

Don't sort your clean linen into separate piles of sheets and pillowcases. Keep matching sets together to use, wash and fade evenly. Save time by labeling single and double sheets before you fold them, so that you can tell them apart. In a corner, sew on a tag of color-coded ribbon. Try pink for single, blue for double.

Tie lilac ribbon around each bundle with a couple of dried lavender stalks inside the bow.

Buying Bed Linen

"Love is like linen. Often changed, the sweeter."
TRADITIONAL SAYING

Buy the softest sheets you can afford. In a recent survey of 500 women, 93 percent said they believe that quality sheets result in a better night's sleep. Combed cotton is smoothest and sateen weave is shinier. Choose 100 percent cotton sheets to keep you cool in the summer, and try a set of fuzzy flannel ones to warm up in the winter.

Princesses and perfectionists prefer cool, absorbent linen sheets that last a lifetime and bear their personal monogram. But if you want luxury without quite so much laundry work, buy linen pillowcases and the softest South Sea Island or Egyptian cotton sheets. Egyptian cotton owes its superior durability, luster, and silky feel to its extra-long fiber staple.

When buying sheets, it is commonly believed that you should choose a high thread count, the number of threads to an inch. However, ways of counting threads can vary dramatically between manufacturers. Higher thread counts denote higher quality, durability, and cost. Sheets of 200 or more threads per inch are also softer. All you need to know is that the finest quality cotton is supercale, followed by fine percale, and percale for everyday use.

Polycottons are a mixture of polyester and cotton which shrug off wrinkles but 100 percent cotton sheets are softer and more breathable. There are different grades of cotton, which is determined by the length of its fiber—the longer it is, the more luxurious and durable the grade of cotton.

If you have sensitive skin, stick to untreated, organic cotton, bleached with oxygen-only bleach.

If your sheets are starting to look gray and dull, soak them in a gallon of warm water and eight ounces of white vinegar. Then rinse with cold water. To keep your whites in good condition, add about one third of a cup of white vinegar to your rinse cycle, and you'll find that your laundry comes out brighter and softer. With the proper care, sheets can last you ten to twenty years.

The following measurements are for fitted sheets and will help ensure a proper fit. Manufacturers' sizes may vary slightly, but these dimensions are a good representation of what should be expected. It is also important to know how deep your mattress is, especially as pillow-top and extra deep mattresses have become very common:

TWIN: 39 x 76in/98 x 190cm

TWIN X-LONG: 39 x 80in/98 x 200cm

FULL: 54 x 75in/135 x 187.5cm

QUEEN: 60 x 80in/150 x 200cm

KING: 78 x 80in/195 x 200cm

CAL-KING: 72 x 84in/180 x 210cm

STANDARD DEPTH: 7 to 9in/18 to 23cm

DEEP MATTRESS: 10 to 15in/25 to 37.5cm

EXTRA DEEP: 15in to as deep as 22in/37.5 to 55cm

Recipes for Tired Bed Linen

- To perk up graying or stained sheets, soak in 40fl oz/1.2liters of warm water and 8fl oz/225ml of white wine vinegar. Rinse in cold water.

- For whiter linen, occasionally substitute 1 tbsp washing soda or baking soda for detergent. Bleach naturally by drying in sunlight.

- For softer sheets, add $\frac{1}{4}$ cup/60ml of white wine vinegar to the final rinse.

- For extra white sheets, fill a boilable bag with eggshells and add to the wash.

- To keep colored bedlinen bright, add 1 tsp Epsom salts to the last rinse.

- Starching is making a comeback. It makes sheets beautifully crisp. You can make your own starch by rinsing or spraying sheets with water used to boil pasta, rice, or potatoes. Never starch linen to store as you split the fibers along the folds. Store it loosely folded, and starch when you need it.

"Buy easy-care bedlinen. I have seen so many marriages in trouble because the wife was up late ironing the sheets, not lying between them." STELLA EGERT

Scenting the Bed Linen

When you make a bed, scent the bedlinen to soothe the sleeper or celebrate a special occasion. Lavender is traditionally used, but you can also spray the linen with other aromatherapy oils or dried flowers, infused overnight in boiling water and cooled.

Put your chosen fragrance in a bottle spray, but don't spray directly on the linen. Spray a mist into the air above it so that droplets drift evenly down onto the linen without spotting.

- **Rose or orange water soothes and relaxes inhibitions.**

- **Jasmine and lily evoke adventurous, exotic moods.**

- **Musky oils are masculine and sexual.**

- **Clary Sage encourages a feeling of well-being and induces vivid dreams.**

- **Sandalwood can lift depressed feelings.**

- **Citrus scents will clear the head during heat spells or times of examination nerves.**

- To help prevent nightmares, place a sprig of rosemary under the pillow.

- To bring good dreams, lay a nutmeg under your pillow.

- To reassure a child who is afraid of monsters, the herb dill will chase away evil witches. Place under the pillow, under the bed, and in the wardrobe. Tell the child or the charm will not work.

"Chanel N° 5"

MARILYN MONROE,
when asked what she wore in bed

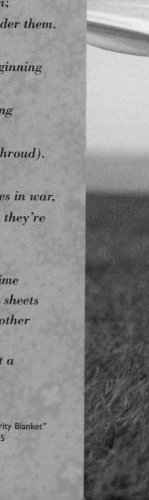

Sheets are fraught with
    meaning…We cover the
    baby with them;
    hide nudity under them.

Sheets are the beginning
    and the end:
    our first clothing
    (swaddling),
    and our last (shroud).

They are bandages in war,
    and rags when they're
    worn out…

We spend more time
    in contact with sheets
    than with any other
    item we own;
    they are almost a
    second skin.

JOAN KRON,
"Sheets: The New Security Blanket"
New York, 24 March 1975

The Well-Made Bed

c

"No one ever died from sleeping in an unmade bed. I have known mothers who remake the bed after their children do it because there is a wrinkle in the spread or the blanket is on crooked. This is sick." ERMA BOMBECK

It may well be pernickity, but there are millions of folk who loath a wrinkled bed. Accordingly, those bed makers who are obsessed with perfection can learn the precise art from the writings of Victorian authors Catherine E. Beecher and Harriet Beecher Stowe (*The American Woman's Home*, 1869) who gave well-defined instructions on how this task should be accomplished:

"Few servants will make a bed properly, without much attention from the mistress of the family; and every young woman who expects to have a household of her own to manage should be able to do it well herself, and to instruct others in doing it. The following directions should be given to those who do this work:

Open the windows, and lay off the bed-covering on two chairs, at the foot of the bed. If it be a feather-bed, after it is well aired, shake the feathers from each corner to the middle; then take up the middle, shake it well, and turn the bed over. Then push the feathers in place, making the head higher than the foot, and the sides even, and as high as the middle part. A mattress, whether used on top of a feather-bed or by itself, should in like manner be well aired and turned. Then put on the bolster and the under sheet, so that the wrong side of the sheet shall go next the bed, and the marking always come at the head, tucking in all around. Then put on the pillows, evenly, so that the open ends shall come to the sides of the bed, and spread on the upper sheet so that the wrong side shall be next the blankets, and the marked end always at the head. This arrangement of sheets is to prevent the part where the feet lie from being reversed, so as to come to the face; and also to prevent the parts soiled by the body from coming to the bedtick and blankets. Put on the other covering, except the outer one, tucking in all around, and then turn over the upper sheet at the head, so as to show a part of the pillows. When the pillow-cases are clean and smooth, they look best outside of the cover, but not otherwise.

Then draw the hand along the side of the pillows, to make an even indentation, and then smooth and shape the whole outside. A nice housekeeper always notices the manner in which a bed is made; and in some parts of the country, it is rare to see this work properly performed."

"*Good morning luvvy! Well, both dogs slept in my room and did not move all night.*"

ALEXANDRA, TSARINA OF RUSSIA, writing to Nicholas II in 1900

Hot Foot

Electric blankets are luxurious in very cold weather and godsends for people who simply get cold feet in bed! They were invented in the early 1900s. At first, they were big and bulky heating devices that were dangerous to use and were considered an oddity.

But in the 1920s, electric blankets started to become more widespread as they were regularly used in tuberculosis sanitariums: tuberculosis patients, who were regularly prescribed plenty of fresh air, used the blankets to keep warm, especially when they slept outdoors.

In 1936 the first electric blanket arrived with a separate thermostat control that automatically turned on and off, in response to room temperature. Later, thermostats were wired into the blankets, until 1984, when thermostat-free electric blankets were introduced. The term "electric blanket" was not used until the 1950s, before which they were referred to as "warming pads" or "heated quilts."

Today, electric blankets come as over- or under-blankets and heated duvets. Some need preheating before bedtime, then are turned off. Don't keep a blanket for more than ten years. Store blankets in the summer by rolling them loosely, and have them professionally checked every three years.

A Much-Loved Bedside Nurse

Robert Louis Stevenson was often sick as a child. As an adult, he used his memories of that time to write poems for children about the pleasures of bed and dreaming. They can be found in his book *A Child's Garden of Verses*, written in 1885, which he dedicated to his devoted nanny.

The Land of Counterpane

WHEN I was sick
  and lay a-bed,
I had two pillows
  at my head,
And all my toys
  beside me lay
To keep me happy
  all the day.

And sometimes for
  an hour or so
I watched my leaden
  soldiers go,
With different uniforms
  and drills,
Among the bed-clothes,
  through the hills;

And sometimes sent
  my ships in fleets
All up and down
  among the sheets;
Or brought my trees
  and houses out,
And planted cities
  all about.

I was the giant
  great and still
That sits upon
  the pillow-hill,
And sees before him,
  dale and plain,
The pleasant land
  of counterpane.

The Lady of the Lamp

"If a patient is cold, if a patient is feverish, if a patient is faint, if he is sick after taking food, if he has a bed-sore, it is generally the fault not of the disease, but of the nursing. I use the word nursing for want of a better. It has been limited to signify little more than the administration of medicines and the application of poultices. It ought to signify the proper use of fresh air, light, warmth, cleanliness, quiet, and the proper selection and administration of diet—all at the least expense of vital power to the patient." from *Notes on Nursing*, Florence Nightingale

Being sick in bed was no fun until Florence Nightingale invented the concept of cossetting the sick in spotless bedrooms. She recommended keeping their spirits up with flowers, get well messages, and bed trays of small, tempting-looking meals. When she went to Scutari, Turkey, to nurse the wounded of the Crimean War, she was appalled by the conditions in which invalids were kept.

She firmly believed that infections came about from dirty and poorly ventilated places. Florence Nightingale campaigned tirelessly to improve health standards at home, work, and in hospitals, publishing 200 books, reports, and pamphlets that continue to be highly regarded in nursing today.

74

The Casualty Clearing Station

GILBERT WATERHOUSE

A bowl of daffodils,
A crimson-quilted bed,
Sheets and pillows white as snow—
White and gold and red—
And sisters moving to and fro,
With soft and silent tread.

So all my spirit fills
With pleasure infinite,
And all the feathered wings of rest
Seem flocking from the radiant West
To bear we thro' the night.

See, how they close me in,
They, and the sisters' arms.
One eye is closed, the other lid
Is watching how my spirit slid
Toward some red-roofed farms,
And having crept beneath them slept
Secure from war's alarms.

Sense and Sensibility

by

JANE AUSTEN

Marianne got up the next morning at her usual time; to every inquiry replied that she was better, and tried to prove herself so, by engaging in her accustomary employments. But a day spent in sitting shivering over the fire with a book in her hand, which she was unable to read, or in lying, weary and languid, on a sofa, did not speak much in favour of her amendment; and when, at last, she went early to bed, more and more indisposed, Colonel Brandon was only astonished at her sister's composure, who, though attending and nursing her the whole day, against Marianne inclination, and forcing proper medicines on her at night, trusted, like Marianne, to the certainty and efficacy of sleep, and felt no real alarm.

A very restless and feverish night, however, disappointed the expectation of both; and when Marianne, after persisting in rising, confessed herself unable to sit up, and returned voluntarily to her bed, Elinor was very ready to adopt Mrs. Jennings's advice, of sending for the Palmers' apothecary.

He came, examined his patient, and though encouraging Miss Dashwood to expect that a very few days would restore her sister to health, yet, by pronouncing her disorder to have a putrid tendency, and allowing the word "infection" to ☞

pass his lips, gave instant alarm to Mrs. Palmer, on her baby's account. Mrs. Jennings, who had been inclined from the first to think Marianne's complaint more serious than Elinor, now looked very grave on Mr. Harris's report, and confirming Charlotte's fears and caution, urged the necessity of her immediate removal with her infant; and Mr. Palmer, though treating their apprehensions as idle, found the anxiety and importunity of his wife too great to be withstood. Her departure, therefore, was fixed on; and within an hour after Mr. Harris's arrival, she set off, with her little boy and his nurse, for the house of a near relation of Mr. Palmer's, who lived a few miles on the other side of Bath; whither her husband promised, at her earnest entreaty, to join her in a day or two; and whither she was almost equally urgent with her mother to accompany her. Mrs. Jennings, however, with a kindness of heart which made Elinor really love her, declared her resolution of not stirring from Cleveland as long as Marianne remained ill, and of endeavouring, by her own attentive care, to supply to her the place of the mother she had taken her from; and Elinor found her on every occasion a most willing and active helpmate, desirous to share in all her fatigues, and often by her better experience in nursing, of material use.

…The comfort of such a friend at that moment as Colonel Brandon – or such a companion for her mother, – how gratefully was it felt! – a companion whose judgment would guide, whose attendance must relieve, and whose friendship might soothe her! – as far as the shock of such a summons could be lessened to her, his presence, his manners, his assistance, would lessen it.

He, meanwhile, whatever he might feel, acted with all the firmness of a collected mind, made every necessary arrangement with the utmost despatch, and calculated with exactness the time in which she might look for his return. Not a moment was lost in delay of any kind. The horses arrived, even before they were expected, and Colonel Brandon only pressing her hand with a look of solemnity, and a few words spoken too low to reach her ear, hurried into the carriage. It was then about twelve o'clock, and she returned to her sister's apartment to wait for the arrival of the apothecary, and to watch by her the rest of the night. It was a night of almost equal suffering to both. Hour after hour passed away in sleepless pain and delirium on Marianne's side, and in the most cruel anxiety on Elinor's, before Mr. Harris appeared. Her apprehensions once raised, paid by their excess for all her former security; and the servant who sat up with her, for she would not allow Mrs. Jennings to be called, only tortured her more, by hints of what her mistress had always thought.

Marianne's ideas were still, at intervals, fixed incoherently on her mother, and whenever she mentioned her name, it gave a pang to the heart of poor Elinor, who, reproaching herself for having trifled with so many days of illness, and wretched for some immediate relief, fancied that all relief might soon be in vain, that every thing had been delayed too long, and pictured to herself her suffering mother arriving too late to see ☞

☞ this darling child, or to see her rational.

She was on the point of sending again for Mr. Harris, or if he could not come, for some other advice, when the former – but not till after five o'clock – arrived. His opinion, however, made some little amends for his delay, for though acknowledging a very unexpected and unpleasant alteration in his patient, he would not allow the danger to be material, and talked of the relief which a fresh mode of treatment must procure, with a confidence which, in a lesser degree, was communicated to Elinor. He promised to call again in the course of three or four hours, and left both the patient and her anxious attendant more composed than he had found them.

With strong concern, and with many reproaches for not being called to their aid, did Mrs. Jennings hear in the morning of what had passed. Her former apprehensions, now with greater reason restored, left her no doubt of the event; and though trying to speak comfort to Elinor, her conviction of her sister's danger would not allow her to offer the comfort of hope. Her heart was really grieved. The rapid decay, the early death of a girl so young, so lovely as Marianne, must have struck a less interested person with concern. On Mrs. Jennings's compassion she had other claims. She had been for three months her companion, was still under her care, and she was known to have been greatly injured, and long unhappy. The distress of her sister too, particularly a favourite, was before her; – and as for their mother, when Mrs. Jennings considered that Marianne might probably be to her what Charlotte was to herself, her sympathy in her sufferings was very sincere.

Mr. Harris was punctual in his second visit; – but he came to be disappointed in his hopes of what the last would produce. His medicines had failed; – the fever was unabated; and Marianne only more quiet – not more herself – remained in a heavy stupor. Elinor, catching all, and more than all, his fears in a moment, proposed to call in further advice. But he judged it unnecessary: he had still something more to try, some more fresh application, of whose success he was as confident as the last, and his visit concluded with encouraging assurances which reached the ear, but could not enter the heart of Miss Dashwood. She was calm, except when she thought of her mother; but she was almost hopeless; and in this state she continued till noon, scarcely stirring from her sister's bed, her thoughts wandering from one image of grief, one suffering friend to another, and her spirits oppressed to the utmost by the conversation of Mrs. Jennings, who scrupled not to attribute the severity and danger of this attack to the many weeks of previous indisposition which Marianne's disappointment had brought on. Elinor felt all the reasonableness of the idea, and it gave fresh misery to her reflections.

About noon, however, she began – but with a caution – a dread of disappointment which for some time kept her silent even to her friend – to fancy, to hope she could perceive a slight amendment in her sister's pulse: she waited, watched, and examined it again and again; and at last, with an ☞

agitation more difficult to bury under exterior calmness than all her foregoing distress, ventured to communicate her hopes. Mrs. Jennings, though forced, on examination, to acknowledge a temporary revival, tried to keep her young friend from indulging a thought of its continuance; and Elinor, coming over every injunction of distrust, told herself likewise not to hope. But it was too late. Hope had already entered; and feeling all its anxious flutter, she bent over her sister to watch – she hardly knew for what. Half an hour passed away, and the favourable symptom yet blessed her. Others even arose to confirm it. Her breath, her skin, her lips, all flattered Elinor with signs of amendment; and Marianne fixed her eyes on her with a rational, though languid, gaze. Anxiety and hope now oppressed her in equal degrees, and left her no moment of tranquillity till the arrival of Mr. Harris at four o'clock; when his assurances, his felicitations on a recovery in her sister even surpassing his expectation, gave her confidence, comfort, and tears of joy.

Marianne was in every respect materially better; and he declared her entirely out of danger. Mrs. Jennings, perhaps satisfied with the partial justification of her forebodings which had been found in their late alarm, allowed herself to trust in his judgment, and admitted, with unfeigned joy, and soon with unequivocal cheerfulness, the probability of an entire recovery.

Elinor could not be cheerful. Her joy was of a different kind, and led to any thing rather than to gaiety. Marianne, restored to life, health, friends, and to her doting mother, was an idea to fill her heart with sensations of exquisite comfort, and expand it in fervent gratitude; but it lead to no outward demonstrations of joy, no words, no smiles. All within Elinor's breast was satisfaction, silent and strong.

She continued by the side of her sister, with little intermission, the whole afternoon; calming every fear, satisfying every enquiry of her enfeebled spirits, supplying every succour, and watching almost every look and every breath. The possibility of a relapse would, of course, in some moments, occur to remind her of what anxiety was; but when she saw, on her frequent and minute examination, that every symptom of recovery continued, and saw Marianne at six o'clock sink into a quiet, steady, and to all appearance comfortable, sleep, she silenced every doubt.

…At seven o'clock, leaving Marianne still sweetly asleep, she joined Mrs. Jennings in the drawing-room to tea. Of breakfast she had been kept by her fears, and of dinner by their sudden reverse, from eating much; and the present refreshment. therefore, with such feelings of content as she brought to it, was particularly welcome. Mrs. Jennings would have persuaded her, at its conclusion, to take some rest before her mother's arrival, and allow her to take her place by Marianne; but Elinor had no sense of fatigue, no capability of sleep at that moment about her, and she was not to be kept away from her sister an unnecessary instant. Mrs. Jennings, therefore, attending her up stairs into the sick chamber, to satisfy herself that all continued right, left her there again to her charge and her thoughts, and retired to her own room to write letters and sleep.

Sleep-Talking

A friend of the author's once sleepwalked onto the balcony of her apartment, naked, to sleep-talk about the plumber to two female neighbors, as they chatted on an adjoining balcony. This happily-married lawyer's wife could not remember her sleep outing in the morning, until the neighbors good-naturedly teased her about the mythical plumber.

Sleep-talkers carry on conversations, moan or make other sounds. Some might suddenly sit up in bed and say something urgent—in words no one else can understand. Others sing eerie and tuneless songs. They have no memory of doing it when awakened.

No one knows why sleep-talking occurs, but it can be associated with sleep deprivation, or feeling feverish or anxious.

If you sleep-talk, keep to a regular bedtime schedule and don't eat heavily before bedtime.

If you have to wake up a sleep-talker, do it gently and reassure them that they are safe.

Snoring

The oldest anti-snoring device is to sew a button on the back of noisy sleepers' pajamas so they don't want to lie on their back.

One in ten men over 40 snores, holding their breath for at least ten seconds hundreds of times a night. What causes it? Lung and heart problems, nasal blockages, allergies, large tonsils, hormonal disorders, alcohol, and medicines are to blame.

Those loud, hoarse, or harsh breathing sounds can break up relationships, condemn you to sleep apart, provoke irritability, and cause sleeplessness.

Basic anti-snoring strategies are to lose weight, never drink alcohol before bed and—it works for some—place a telephone directory under the top of the bed to tilt it.

Pharmacists sell disposable pads that fit over the nose, slightly widening the nostrils. Other devices strap to your wrists, giving a mild shock if you snore—but as they don't discriminate between sounds, talking in bed is likely to be punished as well! Doctors can prescribe sleep masks to increase your oxygen flow, or laser operations to improve the problem. Consult your local sleep clinic.

In Massachusetts, we hear it is illegal to snore unless your windows are closed and locked!

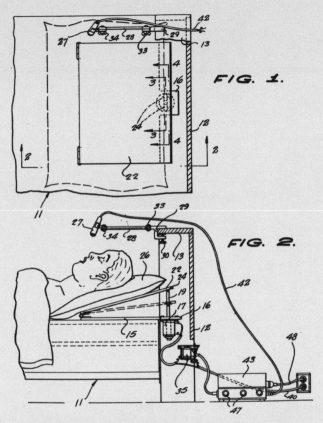

George J. Wilson's 1962 invention for a snore
alarm works by monitoring noise levels with a
microphone and adjusting the angle of the
sleeper's head when snoring is detected.

PATENT NO. 3089130

Wee Willie Winkie

Runs through
    the town,

Upstairs and
    downstairs

In his nightgown.

Rapping at the
    windows,

Crying through
    the lock,

"Are the children
    all in bed?

For it's now eight
    o'clock."

Baby's Room

When decorating a newborn's room, choose soothing pastels for walls: flashy colors such as red stimulate and wake up the baby. Use natural, low-fume paint. Friezes are fun, though don't expect a baby to know the alphabet because you have put it up by his bed! Classical music, played in the bedroom, soothes a baby and is said to increase intelligence.

Stuffed toys and comfort blankets are a baby's most important possessions, as they represent security. If a child has a special cuddly toy, buy several identical ones, in case it is lost.

Don't use pillows or duvets for several years, as they can be dangerous for babies. Make sure the crib's mattress fits snugly without any gaps so the baby can't slip between the cracks and the crib sides. And to reduce the chances of crib death, put the baby to sleep on his back in a crib with a firm, flat mattress, with no soft bedding underneath. You should also be cautious about baby sleeping bags, which button on over the shoulders. Some say they help babies to sleep by stopping them from kicking the bedclothes off. But they may be too hot and tiny infants can slip down inside them. A few thin blankets allow more air through.

Check the temperature with a room thermometer. Some babycare experts advise keeping a bedroom at 68°F/20°C for a clothed baby with a blanket, while wakeful babies cry 👉

☞ less when the temperature is 75°F/24°C, but consider medical advice. Parents can buy sensor pads to monitor a baby's movements, in addition to listening and viewing devices,

Once the baby can sit up, from three months, he needs a drop-sided crib. This is the time when proud parents go to town on a child's bedroom, with themed curtains, wallpaper, lights and sheets. Line the crib with a "bumper" or long thin quilt around the sides, which makes the crib draft-proof and stops the baby hurting himself against the crib sides, but tie it with a knot and secure the ties away from the baby to stop him from undoing them.

Baby activity centres and moving toys are wonderful for early-waking babies. But don't fix them where the baby can use them as a foothold to climb out of the crib!

When the baby can climb out of his crib, or well before a new baby is born, promote him to a bed with safety rails to stop him from rolling out. If you reuse his crib for a new baby, paint it a different color so he doesn't feel the baby has "stolen" his crib. It may be better value to buy a standard single bed than a smaller junior bed. You can also buy Scandinavian sleighbed-style cribs that adapt into beds and then sofas for teenagers.

Don't give children your old mattress. Young bones that are still forming need firm support. If a child wets the bed, disposable bedpads are more comfortable than plastic sheeting.

MAKE A MOBILE FOR A BABY'S COT

A mobile, hung from the cradle hood or above a crib, where the baby can't reach it, will entertain him and help him to focus his eyes. Older babies love musical mobiles, but for your peace, buy one that plays various tunes, not the same one again and again!

Instructions:

• **Take two coat hangers. Tape together crosswise or unpick the metal and twist together. Hide the join with ribbon or tape.**

• From the coat-hanger bottoms, use string or ribbon to tie items at different lengths. Draw simple shapes and faces with thick black pen on white card. Add small toys, balloons, cut-outs from magazines, sweet wrappers, clean yogurt pots— whatever you like. Vary them every few days.

• **Remember to hang objects so that the interesting parts face downward toward the baby's face. A good tip is to use a budgerigar's mirror from a pet shop, so the baby can see himself.**

• Hang the mobile out of the baby's reach, using string or, for a magical "hovering" effect, clear fishing line.

The Lullaby

From inside the womb, we recognize our mother's voice and may even have favorite music. When we are born, lullabies are a link to that voice, and we respond to them even before we can see properly.

For many babies, especially colicky ones, the monotony of an external noise is especially soothing. Singing lullabies is one of the oldest, most natural forms of interaction between parents and babies and can calm an infant not only to sleep, but also in distressing situations like being changed. Some babies like to be wrapped up firmly when sung to, replicating the protection of the womb; others, especially with colic, respond to the "tree leopard" position, lying stomach down and arms and legs dangling along your horizontal arm. Never stop singing, even if you sing nonsense or phrases like "please don't cry." These early feelings of warmth and togetherness form the basis of baby's first attachment and provide the framework for the developing relationship between parent and child.

Brahms' popular lullaby was a variation on an Austrian folk song that Brahms wrote for the first child of his Viennese friend, Berta Porubszky.

Brahms' Lullaby

Lullaby and good night, with roses bedight
With lilies o'er spread is baby's wee bed
Lay thee down now and rest, may thy slumber be blessed
Lay thee down now and rest, may thy slumber be blessed

Lullaby and good night, thy mother's delight
Bright angels beside my darling abide
They will guard thee at rest, thou shalt wake on my breast
They will guard thee at rest, thou shalt wake on my breast.

Original Text for Brahms' Lullaby

GUTEN ABEND, GUTE NACHT,
  MIT ROSEN BEDACHT,

MIT NÄGLEIN BESTECKT,
  SCHLUPF UNTER DIE DECK'

MORGEN FRÜH, WENN GOTT
  WILL, WIRST DU WIEDER
  GEWECKT

MORGEN FRÜH, WENN GOTT
  WILL, WIRST DU WIEDER
  GEWECKT

GUTEN ABEND, GUTE NACHT,
  VON ENGLEIN BEWACHT

DIE ZEIGEN IM TRAUM,
  DIR CHRISTKINDLEINS BAUM

SCHLAF NUN SELIG UND SÜSS,
  SCHAU IM TRAUM'S
  PARADIES

SCHLAF NUN SELIG UND SÜSS,
  SCHAU IM TRAUM'S
  PARADIES

RIGHT: Brahms meets two children,
by A. Schubert

Hush Little Baby

HUSH, LITTLE BABY,
DON'T SAY A WORD.
PAPA'S GONNA BUY YOU
A MOCKINGBIRD

AND IF THAT MOCKINGBIRD
WON'T SING,
PAPA'S GONNA BUY YOU
A DIAMOND RING

AND IF THAT DIAMOND
RING TURNS BRASS,
PAPA'S GONNA BUY YOU
A LOOKING GLASS

AND IF THAT LOOKING
GLASS GETS BROKE,
PAPA'S GONNA BUY YOU
A BILLY GOAT

AND IF THAT BILLY GOAT
WON'T PULL,
PAPA'S GONNA BUY YOU
A CART AND BULL

AND IF THAT CART AND
BULL FALL DOWN,
YOU'LL STILL BE THE
SWEETEST LITTLE BABY
IN TOWN.

Golden Slumbers

GOLDEN SLUMBER
KISS YOUR EYES,
SMILES AWAIT YOU
WHEN YOU RISE.
SLEEP, PRETTY BABY,
DO NOT CRY,
AND I'LL SING YOU
A LULLABY.

CARE YOU KNOW NOT,
THEREFORE SLEEP,
WHILE I O'ER YOU
WATCH DO KEEP.
SLEEP, PRETTY DARLING,
DO NOT CRY,
AND I WILL SING
A LULLABY.

B.BAUCOUR

Publications
François Tédesco
Paris.

99

Twinkle, Twinkle, Little Star

TWINKLE, TWINKLE, LITTLE STAR
HOW I WONDER WHAT YOU ARE!
UP ABOVE THE WORLD SO HIGH
LIKE A DIAMOND IN THE SKY
TWINKLE, TWINKLE, LITTLE STAR
HOW I WONDER WHAT YOU ARE.

All the Pretty Horses

HUSH-A-BYE, DON'T YOU CRY
GO TO SLEEP-Y, LITTLE BABY.
WHEN YOU WAKE YOU SHALL HAVE
ALL THE PRETTY LITTLE HORSES.
BLACKS AND BAYS, DAPPLES AND GRAYS,
COACH AND SIX-A-LITTLE HORSES.
HUSH-A-BYE, DON'T YOU CRY,
GO TO SLEEP-Y, LITTLE BABY.

Frère Jacques

FRÈRE JACQUES, FRÈRE JACQUES,
DORMEZ-VOUS? DORMEZ-VOUS?
SONNEZ LES MATINES, SONNEZ LES MATINES
DING DING DONG, DING DING DONG.

Lavender's Blue (Dilly Dilly)

LAVENDER'S BLUE, DILLY DILLY,
LAVENDER'S GREEN
WHEN YOU ARE KING, DILLY DILLY,
I SHALL BE QUEEN

> WHO TOLD YOU SO, DILLY DILLY,
> WHO TOLD YOU SO?
> 'TWAS MY OWN HEART, DILLY DILLY,
> THAT TOLD ME SO

CALL UP YOUR FRIENDS, DILLY, DILLY
SET THEM TO WORK
SOME TO THE PLOUGH, DILLY DILLY,
SOME TO THE FORK

> SOME TO THE HAY, DILLY DILLY,
> SOME TO THRESH CORN
> WHILST YOU AND I, DILLY DILLY,
> KEEP OURSELVES WARM

LAVENDER'S BLUE, DILLY DILLY,
LAVENDER'S GREEN
WHEN YOU ARE KING, DILLY DILLY,
I SHALL BE QUEEN

> WHO TOLD YOU SO, DILLY DILLY,
> WHO TOLD YOU SO?
> 'TWAS MY OWN HEART, DILLY DILLY,
> THAT TOLD ME SO.

Sleep, Baby, Sleep

SLEEP, BABY, SLEEP
YOUR FATHER TENDS THE SHEEP
YOUR MOTHER SHAKES THE DREAMLAND TREE
AND SOFTLY FALL SWEET DREAMS FOR THEE,
SLEEP, BABY, SLEEP.

Rock-a-bye Baby

ROCK-A-BYE BABY ON THE TREE TOP
WHEN THE WIND BLOWS THE CRADLE WILL ROCK;
WHEN THE BOUGH BREAKS THE CRADLE WILL FALL,
DOWN WILL COME BABY, CRADLE AND ALL.

Baby Beds

LITTLE LAMBS, LITTLE LAMBS,
WHERE DO YOU SLEEP?
"IN THE GREEN MEADOW
WITH MOTHER SHEEP."

LITTLE BIRDS, LITTLE BIRDS,
WHERE DO YOU REST?
"CLOSE TO OUR MOTHER
IN A WARM NEST."

BABY DEAR, BABY DEAR,
WHERE DO YOU LIE?
"IN MY WARM BED
WITH MOTHER CLOSE BY."

Bye Baby Bunting

BYE BABY BUNTING
DADDY'S GONE A'HUNTING,
MUMMY'S GONE A'MILKING,
SISTER'S GONE A'SILKING,
BROTHER'S GONE TO BUY A SKIN
TO WRAP THE BABY BUNTING IN.

It is every baby's birthright to own a teddy bear. Bears are devoted to comforting their owners. In return, they are cherished for a lifetime and passed down through families.

Lovable Bed Companions

Sensible people know that, like Santa Claus, the teddy bear has always been around. However, others tell a story that begins in 1902, when President Theodore "Teddy" Roosevelt refused to shoot a bear cub while on a four-day hunt in Mississippi. Clifford Berryman, a newspaper cartoonist, recorded the event in one of his drawings, and it was later published on the front of *The Washington Post*. Readers of the paper were delighted, and eager to see more of the bear. Morris Michtom, a Russian immigrant living in New York, asked his wife Rose to make a toy bear based on the drawing. The creature was instantly popular, and in response to the huge demand, Morris and Rose Michtom set up their own toy-making company, the Ideal Novelty and Toy Company.

About the same time, Richard Steiff, nephew of Margarete, a then upcoming German felt toy-maker, proposed extending their repertoire from elephants to mohair jointed bears and monkeys, hoping to appeal more to boys. He recalled that his aunt "did not place too much hope on the success of the bear because of its high price." But when an American department-store sales agent saw them, he ordered three thousand. He realized the eternal truth: teddies are an overnight ☞

success. In 1920, the adventurous, magical Rupert Bear was born in cartoon form. Literary star Winnie the Pooh appeared in 1926, and Paddington Bear traveled to London from Darkest Peru in 1958.

Adults love teddies, too. Odes to the teddy bear are proof positive: singers from Elvis Presley to Jerry Garcia and The Grateful Dead have pledged their love to the furry creature.

Serious collectors prize Steiff bears, with their trademark button in their ear. Colonel Bob Henderson's Steiff, Teddy Girl, fetched £110,000 ($171,600) at auction in London—and its proud new owner flew her home to Japan in a separate first class seat.

The teddy bear has even survived world-famous disasters. Polar the Titanic Bear was such a creature. American heiress Daisy Corning Stone Spedden wrote this well-known story for her son Douglas after they escaped the sinking of the Titanic.

Monaco Bear currently stands as the most expensively priced bear in the world. The Steiff bear was dressed by Louis Vuitton in the famous monogram-print raincoat, hat, and matching luggage and auctioned off to raise money for charity. He was sold for $190,000 in October 2000.

Make a Teddy Bear

To make your own $3\frac{1}{2}$ in/9cm traditional bear, you will need:

MATERIALS
- Small piece of mohair with $\frac{1}{8}$in/3mm pile, or upholstery velvet or other fabric of your choice
- Tiny piece of leather or ultrasuede for pads
- Two black beads for eyes
- Thread to match fur, plus black thread for nose and mouth
- Stuffing (cotton wool would suffice)
- Five sets of cotter pin joints (available by mail order from suppliers of bear-making components)
- Scraps of ribbon or lace to trim

TOOLS
- Small embroidery scissors
- Needle
- Narrow-nosed pliers (for turning cotter pins in the joints)
- Stuffing stick (such as a small wooden nail-care stick)

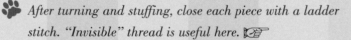

GENERAL GUIDELINES

 Always place the right sides of the fabric together before stitching.

 Tack the pieces first with a tiny running stitch, then use a strong back stitch for the permanent seams.

Make sure the stuffing goes right into the extremities.

After turning and stuffing, close each piece with a ladder stitch. "Invisible" thread is useful here. 👉

To cut out:

1. Trace the pattern pieces and transfer to card.
2. Make sure that the pile of the fabric runs downward, as indicated by the arrows, before placing the pattern pieces on the back of the fabric. Cut out.

To make the bear's head:

1. Tack and backstitch from A down to B.
2. Position the gusset with a tacking stitch at A.
3. Sew from A around to C on one side of the gusset and then on the other, leaving the neck edge B to C open for stuffing the head.
4. Join the two ear pieces together by sewing round the curve, leaving the straight edge open between D and D for turning. Turn the ear and then close the opening. Repeat for the second ear.

To make the body:

1. Sew the curved edges together between E and F.
2. Join the back pieces to the front from G to F.
3. Stitch from H to F, leaving an opening as indicated.

To make the arms (2):

1. Sew paw pad to inner arm along straight edge.
2. Join inner arm to outer arm, leaving an opening as indicated.

To make the legs (2):

1. With right sides together, sew around the legs from the toe to the back of the heel, leaving an opening as shown. Do not sew across the straight lower edge of the foot.
2. Fit the foot pad, catching it in place at the toe and heel before tacking and then stitching.

To make up the bear:

1. Stuff the head.
2. Place cotter pin joint in neck opening and close with running stitch.
3. Position joints in arms and legs. Stuff the limbs.
4. Close openings in the limbs with a ladder stitch.
5. Attach the head and limbs to the body using the cotter pin joints.
6. Stuff the body and close the opening.
7. Sew the ears in position with a firm ladder stitch.
8. Sew in the eyes and stitch the nose and mouth.
9. Trim with lace or ribbon as desired. ☞

These templates are actual size.

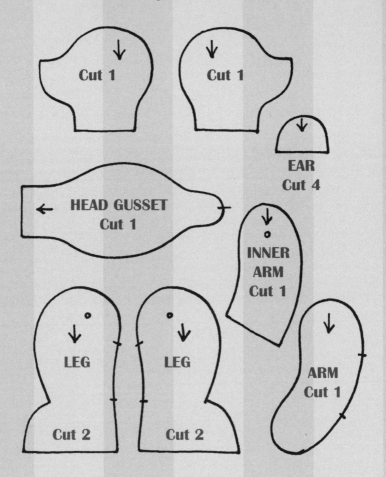

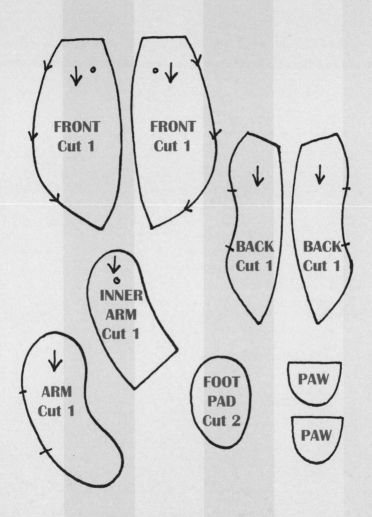

FRONT
Cut 1

FRONT
Cut 1

BACK
Cut 1

BACK
Cut 1

INNER
ARM
Cut 1

ARM
Cut 1

FOOT
PAD
Cut 2

PAW

PAW

Moses Baskets

Moses gave his name to a baby's first woven basket bed. The Bible recounts how his mother hid him as an infant, because the King of Egypt had decreed that all Hebrew boys were to be drowned in the Nile. But when Moses was too big to continue hiding, his mother placed him in a woven, watertight basket in the grass at the edge of the river. Luckily, the King's daughter found him and adopted him.

Moses baskets, prettily padded against drafts, with frills and shady hoods, are cosier than cribs for a newborn and make it easy to carry a baby around. If you reuse a basket for a new baby, always buy a brand new mattress with breathable holes and made of foam guaranteed not to emit toxic fumes. Some people place a sheepskin under the baby for comfort, but others advise against it until the baby is older, in case he breathes in fibers.

Moses baskets and cribs are designed for a baby's first few months. They're not essential, but they do provide a comforting environment. Make sure the one you use is fire resistant, and many experts advise against putting the basket on the floor. If you have a cat, buy a cat-proof cover for the basket. This must have large holes like a tennis net, which make it hard for the cat to walk on it, rather than a tiny mesh, which can support a sleeping animal comfortably.

Fais dodo, Colas mon p'tit frère
Fais dodo, t'auras du lolo
Maman est en haut
Qui fait des gateaux
Papa est en bas
Qui fait du chocolat
Fait dodo Colas mon p'tit frère
Fait dodo, t'auras du lolo.

Go to sleep, Colas my little brother
Go to sleep, you will have your milk
Mummy is upstairs
Making cakes
Daddy is downstairs
Making chocolate
Go to sleep, Colas my little brother
Go to sleep, you will have your milk.

Food for Happy Dreams

If midnight munchies are your bedtime pastime, here's some excellent advice: "breakfast like a king, lunch like a prince, and dine like a pauper." It may even help you to have happy dreams!

Lighter meals are more likely to give you a restful night's sleep. High-fat meals and large servings prolong the work of your digestive system, and all the gas production and rumblings may keep you awake. Some people find that highly-seasoned foods (e.g., hot peppers and garlic) interfere with sleep, especially if you suffer from heartburn. Going to bed with a full stomach does not generally promote a restful night's sleep. While you may fall asleep faster, all the intestinal work required to digest a big meal is likely to cause frequent waking and a poorer quality of sleep. Eat your evening meal early or make lunch your main meal of the day.

A high-fiber diet, loaded with nutrient-rich fruits and vegetables and low in fat improves your general health and helps foster sleep.

B-vitamins, zinc, copper, and iron are linked with sound sleep, and tryptophan-laden foods, such as dairy products and meat, can have a sedative effect. It takes around one hour for the tryptophan in the foods to reach the brain, so don't wait until right before bedtime to have your snack. Carbohydrates trigger the brain chemical serotonin, which makes you sleepy. Some good bedtime snacks to have are:

- **apple pie and ice cream**
- **whole-grain cereal with milk**
- **hazelnuts**
- **tofu**
- **oatmeal-raisin cookies, and a glass of milk**
- **peanut butter sandwich**
- **ground sesame seeds**
- **yogurt, dates, and figs**

Avoid foods such as soft cheese, spinach, tomatoes, and processed meats containing the energizing amino acid tyramine. Limit tea, coffee, caffeinated drinks, and cigarettes. Alcohol makes you wake up feeling tired and dehydrated.

A proper breakfast restores your body's glucose levels after sleep, helping you to concentrate. Asian and Siberian ginseng, Reishi mushrooms—a 5,000-year-old tonic in China—and a herb called rhodiola can help to maintain normal levels of an energy-giving hormone called cortisol.

There was an Old Person of Rheims,

who was troubled with horrible dreams;

So to keep him awake they fed him with cake,

Which amused that Old Person of Rheims.

EDWARD LEAR

Bedroom Cocktails

"His voice was as intimate as the rustle of sheets."

DOROTHY PARKER

BETWEEN THE SHEETS

Cool your glass for several hours in the fridge. Crush ice by wrapping it in a dish towel and smashing with a meat mallet or hammer.

Into a cocktail shaker filled with crushed ice, pour:

- **One part brandy**
- **One part Cointreau**
- **One part Benedictine**
- **Juice of one lemon**
- **Sugar to taste**

Shake. Serve.

NOT TONIGHT JOSEPHINE

- **3 parts red wine**
- **1 part Napoleon Brandy**
- **Dash of Pernod**

Pour the red
wine into a brandy
glass with a couple
of ice cubes.

Add the brandy and Pernod.

Stir, and garnish with
cocktail onions and a
maraschino cherry.

Grandes Horizontales

Until the nineteenth century, courtesans, such as geisha, were the ultimate bedtime luxury for aristocratic men. A man would lavish a fortune on jewels for a woman, but her sexual favors were bestowed when she chose, never bought. One of the most famous courtesans was Mata Hari, the Dutch dancer and spy of World War I, who courted many military officers and was eventually executed by the French for espionage.

Harriette Wilson was the mistress of the Duke of Wellington and a notorious "literate courtesan." Eventually she gave up her philandering, moved to Paris, married, and settled down to a literary career. Her infamous *Memoirs* revealed sordid details of her liaisons. When Wellington learned of the book he threatened to sue and uttered the words: "Publish, and be damned!"

Bedroom Farce

Elmire: Bring up this table and get under it.

Orgon: What?

Elmire: One essential is to hide you well.

Orgon: Why under there?

Elmire: Oh dear! Do as I say;
I know what I'm about, as you shall see.
Get under, now, I tell you; and once there
Be careful no one either sees or hears you.

Orgon: I'm going a long way to humor you,
I must say; but I'll see through your scheme.

from *Tartuffe*, Molière

Chekhov called his early farces "jokes in one act." But what exactly is the joke? In Feydeau's farces, respectable bourgeois citizens rush from bed to bed, hysterically seeking sexual pleasure. Inevitably, the object of desire slips through their fingers, and the frustrated seekers plod home—sadder, but no wiser. Duped by desire, they lose their respectability and their money, and we laugh out loud at their silliness. Feydeau has torn the mask off civilization.

The typical farce story line is now well known: ladies in filmy negligees, men in funny pajamas, confused couples, fast comings and goings, and hiding in the wardrobe…a good bedroom romp combines all these. But this is not all about sex, of course: bedroom farce is fuelled by frustration and unrequited desire.

A typical theater set for a farce simply comprises a bedroom with two doors and a wardrobe—as seen in the classic productions of the 1960s, starring Brian Rix. In a succession of plays at the Whitehall Theatre, London, he was usually in another woman's bedroom, trousers down, displaying his trademark red spotted shorts, just as her husband walked in. Movies have tended to stray away from this well-worn formula, but some, like *Pillow Talk* (1959) have a similar mood, with Doris playing the ingenue to Rock Hudson's handsome "wolf."

Farce has been around for thousands of years, and in many different guises, ranging from Aristophanes to the Marx brothers! Also, it's an immensely versatile form, which is now used to great effect on TV—for instance, Frasier frequently uses bedroom farce plots, with brilliant and memorable results. With its zany humor, wild antics, slapstick, pratfalls, and misunderstandings, the appeal of farce is eternal—the show's guaranteed to run and run!

"...Here he comes. Keep still don't show yourself."

The Bedroom Slipper

By the end of the day, we all long to slip into something more comfortable than our day shoes. Some people never take their slippers off. Hugh Hefner, founder of *Playboy* magazine, wears his trademark silk pajamas and bedroom slippers every day, and works from his bed.

There is no keepsake more sentimental than a tiny baby's slipper, and some parents have them covered in silver. Children's slippers are crazy and oversized, decorated with soft toy cartoon heroes like Garfield, king of sleepy cats.

Sophisticated, plush slippers, monogrammed with one's coat of arms, cost hundreds. More to Scottish tastes are lambswool-lined deerskin moccasins which last years, while in Kenya, bedroom flipflops are made from recycled tyres.

Greek bright felt slippers with raffish pompoms are extremely popular. Colder countries favor knitted knee-high slippersocks.

Vietnamese slippers are unique: unisex open jute sandals with waterhyacinth braids, dusted with cinnamon powder, an old ayurvedic foot-refresher.

Slippers can be the height of seductiveness. Pink feather-trimmed high-heeled mules exude flirtatious femininity.

A Bedtime Indulgence

LUXURY HOT CHOCOLATE

*To serve one, in a tall mug,
or two in small cups:*

- 5½oz/150g fine quality bittersweet chocolate (organic is best)
- 1¼ cup/300ml milk
- A vanilla pod or a few cardamom pods, ground
- Dash of your favorite liquor, if wanted
- Marshmallows or 1 tbsp whipped cream
- Small whisk

Break the chocolate up in your favorite bowl. Melt it by gently microwaving or placing over a bowl of boiling water. This is best done away from the stove, as steam could get into the chocolate and spoil it.

Meanwhile put the milk in a pan and add either a vanilla pod or a generous pinch of cardomom.

Gently warm and add a splash of your favorite liquor, if you wish.

Once the milk has almost boiled, remove from the heat and slowly add it to the melted chocolate, whisking gently into a creamy drink.

Dunk marshmallows or spoon the whipped cream on top for maximum pleasure.

At the bottom of the cup will be some warm melted chocolate to finish with a spoon.

Nightcaps

"Surely, I would say, most men do not wear those shocking cotton nightcaps; else all women's illusions had been destroyed on the first night of their marriage!" from Memoirs, Harriette Wilson

Much of our body heat is lost through our head. You feel warmer in a nightcap, as anyone who has ever camped on a cold night will know.

During the 1500s, men and women began wearing "nightbonnets" or "biggins" made of embroidered white linen or silk. The earliest designs buttoned under the chin and were often red, suggesting the idea of warmth. "Let your night cappe have a hole in the top through which the vapour may goe out," suggested William Vaughan in 1602. Wealthy men's nightcaps were velvet-trimmed.

By the eighteenth century, men wore skullcap-style nightcaps with upturned brims to protect their shaved heads when they removed their wigs. Women wore caps to protect their sheets from the oils and pomades they used in their hair—unless they had hairstyles of such elaboration that they had to sleep standing up. Nightcaps started going out of fashion with the younger generation, around 1880.

Silk and Satin Sheets

Legend has it that silk was discovered in 2640B.C. by the Chinese princess Hsi Ling Shi. It is said that a silkworm cocoon fell into her cup of tea; when she removed it, it emerged as a single thread. Silk-harvesting still uses this principle of softening the natural sericin adhesive in boiling water.

Silk fibers are the lightest of all natural fibers. Silk is a natural insulator and breathes very well, keeping you cool in the summer and warm in the winter. Silk fiber is lustrous, smooth, supple, lightweight, elastic, and strong. Silk resists mildews, molds, and rots that attack other fibers.

True satin is made from silk. It is a glossy woven fabric characterized by a smooth, soft slippery texture. Satin has a silk-like luster. The reflections of light by the even, smooth surface of warp threads gives satin its distinctive brilliance and luster.

To flatter their white complexions, ladies such as the famous beauties of Venice slept on black satin sheets.

Silk and satin sheets in amazing "come-hither" colors are sexy and self-indulgent. But even if you just want to eat ice-cream alone in your silken bed, here is a note of practicality: stain removal is hard at the low temperature wash demanded by silk. Synthetic silk washes better but may slide you unromantically off the bed.

Dressed for the Night

Pajamas for women had became highly fashionable during the 1920s—probably as a reaction against the ultra-feminine frou-frou and frills of Edwardian nightgowns. Certainly the lingerie of the early twentieth century was immensely romantic. Nightgowns were often more elaborately detailed than street dresses. They were fashioned from delicate ivory silk crepe, trimmed with rows of silk lace, silk ribbon flowers, and silk chiffon roses. Lovingly hand-stitched, with rows of delicate embroidery, these charming nightgowns had a subtle, seductive allure.

Nightdresses had previously been plain and high-collared, and decoration considered immoral. Colored ribbon, frills, and flimsy fabrics were regarded with suspicion. However, by the turn of the century, nightgowns were most certainly designed to entice.

"There is nothing more charming, dainty and comfortable than the robe de nuit of the moment," cooed the Lady's Realm magazine of 1903… "an underlying current of coquetry is permissible in a young and charming bride. Two or three dozen nightdresses are not too many…You should spend a large portion of your trousseau money on these important garments." However much the demure side of femininity was underlined in the buttoned-up brushed nylon creations of the 1950s, the desire for glamorous nightgowns has never truly subsided.

"Cute as candy cane, cozy as a kitten—yet they're comfortable to wear. They're all in wonderful fireside warm 'Dream-glo Interlock' —a girl's best friend come winter."

"'Sweet Dreams to You' with lace on your collar and lace at your wrists. Shirred at bust and waist for flattering fit."

Pajamas

"One morning, I shot an elephant in my pajamas. How he got in my pajamas I don't know." GROUCHO MARX

Made in silk, Noël Coward-style, pajamas are the epitome of cool elegance; but when made in striped, rough textured flannel, they are icons of cozy bedtime comfort.

But how did they come into vogue? As with various clothing items, pajamas were first introduced to Europe by colonialists returning from India and North Africa in the late 1800s. However, Francis Pyrard, a French traveler held captive in Goa in 1608, made the earliest known mention of them by a European. He wrote in his book *Voyage de Francis Pyrard de Lava*, published in 1610, that the

Portuguese residents of that city always wore cotton trousers when going to bed.

This was a great contrast to the usual nighttime garb—traditional linen nightshirts were worn by both men and women right up to the turn of the century. However, by 1898, merchants in London were advertising pajamas as a brand new fashion (the word pajamas literally means "leg clothes"). They were considered more practical and modern than nightshirts.

They were also immensely colorful: gentlemen in the early 1900s bought silk pajamas by the dozen, striped in peacock hues that they could not wear by day.

Interestingly, pajamas developed a kind of "dual use"—they already had their new role as nightwear, but by the 1920s, they had also evolved into a new fashion for women, who wore artificial silk crepe de chine or satin pajamas as sophisticated party or casual wear.

EXTRACT FROM

Following the Equator

by

MARK TWAIN

We left Bombay for Allahabad by a night train. It is the
custom of the country to avoid day travel when it can
conveniently be done. But there is one trouble: while you can
seemingly "secure" the two lower berths by making early
application, there is no ticket as witness of it, and no other
producible evidence in case your proprietorship shall chance
to be challenged. The word "engaged" appears on the
window, but it doesn't state who the compartment is engaged,
for. If your Satan and your Barney arrive before somebody
else's servants, and spread the bedding on the two sofas and
then stand guard till you come, all will be well; but if they
step aside on an errand, they may find the beds promoted to
the two shelves, and somebody else's demons standing guard
over their master's beds, which in the meantime have been
spread upon your sofas.

...It was a long journey—two nights, one day, and part of
another day, from Bombay eastward to Allahabad; but it was
always interesting, and it was not fatiguing. At first the, night
travel promised to be fatiguing, but that was on account of
pyjamas. This foolish night-dress consists of jacket and
drawers. Sometimes they are made of silk, sometimes of a

raspy, scratchy, slazy woolen material with a sandpaper surface. The drawers are loose elephant-legged and elephant-waisted things, and instead of buttoning around the body there is a drawstring to produce the required shrinkage. The jacket is roomy, and one buttons it in front. Pyjamas are hot on a hot night and cold on a cold night—defects which a nightshirt is free from. I tried the pyjamas in order to be in the fashion; but I was obliged to give them up, I couldn't stand them. There was no sufficient change from day-gear to night-gear. I missed the refreshing and luxurious sense, induced by the night-gown, of being undressed, emancipated, set free from restraints and trammels. In place of that, I had the worried, confined, oppressed, suffocated sense of being abed with my clothes on. All through the warm half of the night the coarse surfaces irritated my skin and made it feel baked and feverish, and the dreams which came in the fitful flurries of slumber were such as distress the sleep of the damned, or ought to; and all through the cold other half of the night I could get no time for sleep because I had to employ it all in stealing blankets. But blankets are of no value at such a time; the higher they are piled the more effectively they cork the cold in and keep it from getting out. The result is that your legs are ice, and you know how you will feel by and by when you are buried. In a sane interval I discarded the pyjamas, and led a rational and comfortable life thenceforth.

Personalize Your Slippers

- To decorate a child's plain slippers, use a fuzzy felt toy kit in his or her favorite theme, such as trains or dolls. Sew or glue the cut-outs on the slippers.

- Buy two small cross-stitch embroidery kits—you can find them as greeting-card kits. Some have pictures; others give you the patterns for your initials. Sew one square with the letter M and a second with the letter E. Sew to the front of a plain pair of slippers.

- Sew bells, from craft-supply shops or music shops, on the toes of your slippers, "and you shall have music wherever you go."

- Sew a pair of miniature teddy bears on your slippers, or go psychedelic by painting your slippers with dye paint or laundry-proof pens. Write slogans.

- Go vintage and add a huge rosette to the front of your slippers.

- Pin badges with wacky slogans onto your slippers.

Comfy
Felt
Slippers

Bedtime Beauty Routines

Queen Alexandra of England started the fashion for bedtime beauty regimes. To tempt her notoriously unfaithful husband, Edward VII, back to the marital bed, it is said she had a tattoo drawn in an intimate place.

The idea that "it's your duty to be beautiful" led millions of women to perform pointless pre-bed rituals, like brushing their hair a hundred times, before spending the night in the most unrestful contraptions.

Double chins were firmed using Madame Adair of Bond Street's chin strap. Nostrils were pinched together using a French device to "narrow the nose." At bedtime, pale hands were placed in gloves containing a hand cream of wine, salad oil, and mutton grease. Men waxed and pointed their moustache and protected it with a moustache net.

Later, prickly curlers worn under alluring nylon sleep bonnets and a face smothered in moisturizing cream were surely the greatest contraception aid known to mankind. Straight, natural hairstyles worn by '60s and '70s stars like Marianne Faithfull and Ali McGraw proved the answer to men's bedtime prayers.

Beauty Before Bed

As you sleep, the skin replenishes damage done during the day. That is why the two keys to youthful looks are sleep and a before-bed beauty routine.

Soap and face cloths merely clean your skin. "Cleansing," in beauty-speak, is a deeper, gentler, almost spiritual operation involving creams and faith.

After using a cleanser, a toner closes the skin pores, though it's not for everyone. At last, like a luscious rich pudding course in a dinner, comes the moisturizer. Marilyn Monroe's secret was petroleum jelly, applied repeatedly in very thin layers. But now a bevy of ultra modern products exist to suit every skin type.

To prevent wrinkles forming, apply moisturizer upwards from the neck. Pat it on and leave to soak in.

Research has pinpointed the age at which a woman starts reading skincare adverts as exactly 30. Unlike much advertising, they will read the entire blurb and phone their friends to pass it on if they find a cream that works.

"Personal beauty is a better recommendation than any letter of introduction." ARISTOTLE

The Celestial Bed

If the word "health club" sends you diving back under the duvet, you will be delighted to know that the original health club celebrated the virtues of bed over biceps.

London's Temple of Health was opened in 1779 by quack doctor James Graham. Patrons paid two guineas (approximately £120 or $200 in today's money) to see the Celestial Bed where the scantily-clad teenage Emma Lyon lolled all day beneath the inscription "Be fruitful. Multiply and replenish the Earth." Occasionally, a servant tilted the bed to a new angle, delighting her admirers, especially if they glanced at the nine-foot wide bed's overhead mirror.

Meanwhile, Graham lectured on the bed's amazing qualities. Anyone parting with the £50 (£3,200 or $5,800 in today's money) fee for an overnight stay, without Emma of course, would be "blessed with progeny."

The bed's secrets were a mattress stuffed with the best stallion hair, lavender, and an electrified headboard "calculated to give the necessary degree of strength and exertion to the nerves."

There are no testimonials about the bed's success, but Emma profited from her time as a professional bed-tester. She became Lady Hamilton, and lived in a ménage à trois with her husband and her lover, Admiral Lord Nelson.

Dreams

Dreams are vital for health. Everyone dreams, unless they have a protein deficiency or personality disorder.

You may think you are relaxing, but the average sleeper has a busy time at night. The average sleeper dreams about five dreams, over two hours of sleep a night. Our sleeping bodies progress rapidly through a series of five physical changes, each with different heart rates, temperatures, and movements. We repeat these stages up to seven times each night. Most dreams seem to occur in the fifth stage, Rapid Eye Movement (REM), which starts about half an hour after falling asleep. Our body stays still and our eyes dart around under closed eyelids. "Lucid dreams" happen when you realize you are dreaming in the middle of a dream. Usually you wake up, but some people enjoy directing their dreams' outcome when sleeping.

Some say Vitamin B-6 can help you have more vivid dreams and improve your chances of remembering them. However, if you take too much, you dreams may become so vivid that you find them waking you up. If you have this problem, reduce the amount of B-6 that you are taking.

A Japanese company has invented a product that enables people to create their own dreams. Prospective dreamers are asked to look at a photo of what they would like to dream about and then record a story line into the "dream factory."

The machine uses the voice recording, along with lights, music, and smells, to help people direct dreams during periods of REM sleep.

Sleepers are awakened gently after eight hours with music and lights simulating sunlight so users of the gadget do not forget their dream in the shock of waking.

RIGHT: Three night-flying spirits pour beautiful dreams into the head of a sleeping man.

LE RÊVE

EXTRACT FROM

Dreams

by

JEROME K. JEROME

Another extraordinary dream I had was one in which
I dreamed that I was engaged to be married to my Aunt Jane.
That was not, however, the extraordinary part of it; I have
often known people to dream things like that. I knew a man
who once dreamed that he was actually married to his own
mother-in-law! He told me that never in his life had he loved
the alarm clock with more deep and grateful tenderness than
he did that morning. The dream almost reconciled him to
being married to his real wife. They lived quite happily
together for a few days, after that dream.

No; the extraordinary part of my dream was, that I knew it
was a dream. "What on earth will uncle say to this
engagement?" I thought to myself, in my dream. "There's
bound to be a row about it. We shall have a deal of trouble
with uncle, I feel sure." And this thought quite troubled me
until the sweet reflection came: "Ah! well, it's only a dream."

And I made up my mind that I would wake up as soon as
uncle found out about the engagement, and leave him and
Aunt Jane to fight the matter out between themselves.

It is a very great comfort, when the dream grows troubled
and alarming, to feel that it is only a dream, and to know that

we shall awake soon and be none the worse for it. We can dream out the foolish perplexity with a smile then.

Sometimes the dream of life grows strangely troubled and perplexing, and then he who meets dismay the bravest is he who feels that the fretful play is but a dream—a brief, uneasy dream of three score years and ten, or thereabouts, from which, in a little while, he will awake—at least, he dreams so.

How dull, how impossible life would be without dreams—waking dreams, I mean—the dreams that we call "castles in the air," built by the kindly hands of Hope! Were it not for the mirage of the oasis, drawing his footsteps ever onward, the weary traveler would lie down in the desert sand and die. It is the mirage of distant success, of happiness that, like the bunch of carrots fastened an inch beyond the donkey's nose, seems always just within our reach, if only we will gallop fast enough, that makes us run so eagerly along the road of Life.

Providence, like a father with a tired child, lures us ever along the way with tales and promises, until, at the frowning gate that ends the road, we shrink back, frightened. Then, promises still more sweet he stoops and whispers in our ear, and timid yet partly reassured, and trying to hide our fears, we gather up all that is left of our little stock of hope and, trusting yet half afraid, push out our groping feet into the darkness.

Dream Interpretation

Dreams can reflect our desires, fears, and goals, and can even provide a glimpse into the future. Here is a short list of some common dream themes and what they signify.

Abduction—fear of losing personal space

Ants—a project will need hard work

Autumn—maturity verging on decline, a time of reckoning and change

Baby—new beginning or project

Baby carriage—preoccupation with family relationships

Bathrooms—a visit is a need for self-expression

Beach—a period of emotional change when new feelings are surfacing and old experiences can be washed away

Beggar—a recent generous act may hide feelings of fear or pride

Bell—consider your core values; when you are called to account in your waking life, you will prove your worth

Bicycle—confidence in your own abilities

Birds—freedom

Blue—wisdom or sadness

Brain—mental upheaval; you may also be neglecting your powers of reason in favor of emotional outbursts

Breasts—need to be mothered or sexual arousal

Bull—your passions may be out of control: rise above a stressful situation and remain emotionally detached

Butterflies—a transformation

Cake—a need to share

Cat—unhappiness and bad luck

Celebrities—desire to imitate a hero or beauty

Chocolate—reward yourself

Clock—an important event or deadline is troubling you

Cobwebs—healing and perseverance

Coffee—you may have been led astray by an adversary who seeks to undermine your peace of mind; if you grind coffee you are harboring a grudge

Coins—worldly attachment will cause conflict with a small act of kindness

Crocodile—accepting too many responsibilities will make you unnaturally submissive

Crossroads—making a decision; standing still and turning back are both choices

Crow—monogamy: put aside a superficial union and seek worthwhile company

Cuckoo—feelings of displacement or alienation

Dinosaur—old issues are returning to haunt you

Doctor—good health and prosperity; it also indicates a victorious engagement in business or love

Dog—loyalty and generosity from your friends

Dog (barking)—unexpected news

Dog (growling)—you may be punishing others for your own mistakes

Dolphin—harmony and innocent intentions

Doors—a new stage of life

Duck—a fortunate journey: expect to ascend to a new level of influence

Earthquake—take great care when completing a business deal or concluding a sale or purchase

Elephant—you are laying a firm foundation for achieving wealth or great honors

Face—if flawed, you have suffered an attack on your reputation

Family—harmony if they are happy, gloomy prospects if they are sad

Fairy—you seek advice

Father—authority

Fingernails (clean)—self-respect and good opinion

Fingernails (dirty)—disgrace or avoidance of responsibilities

Firefighter—don't chase risks for the sake of other people's admiration

Fish—if you see fish swimming in

clear waters, you will be favored
by those in positions of power.
If you catch fish, you will
acquire wealth through your
own ingenuity

Flamingo—gregarious enjoyment
of new experiences

Forest—concealed fears and
impulses; or suppressed
childhood ambitions

Fruit—sexual or financial gain

Garden—inner growth

Gardening—skillful financial
management and patient planning

Gold—rewards are coming

Goldfish—good fortune,
prosperity, and beauty

Guests—the unattainable

Hair (long)—fear of growing old;
a corresponding trouble in
business and the need to
determine your real priorities

Hat (lost)—business dealings may
suffer a temporary setback

Hat (new)—a return to
traditional methods after a
period of change

Heart—an imbalance in your
personal life that is blocking love

Hens—petty desires threaten your
dignity and inner balance

Hiccups—someone is thinking of
you and a secret admirer may be
arranging a meeting

Hippopotamus—a voracious
appetite and the application of
unreasonable force; gather friends
with genuine enthusiasm rather
than shows of conspicuous
consumption.

Horse—prosperity and good luck

House—need security

Insects—small annoyances

Jewelry (lost)—you may be
betrayed by a close friend;

Jewelry (received)—good luck and
romantic adventures

Kangaroo—your reputation is
being threatened

Kidnapped—you are in an
embarrassing situation

Koala—self-sufficiency and
meticulous attention to detail

Lighthouse—a need for modesty
in a high position

Leather—wards off bad feeling and ill will and creates new challenges

Lilies—sadness and physical suffering

Locust—a disruption in your prosperity that is linked to migration or travel

Lover (new)—you recognise your personal worth

Lover (old)—unresolved issues

Mistletoe—insight

Monkeys—people wish to trick you with flattery

Moon—death and rebirth, and returning warmth after coldness

Mosquitoes—someone has been monopolizing much of your time and resources by refusing to face facts

Mountain—if you fall or falter on your climb, you will be hindered by envy and lack of faith

Octopus—simplify and practice moderation if you are struggling with several priorities

Ostrich—justice and truth

Overeating—take care that you are not acting outside your legitimate sphere of influence or power

Owl—inner knowledge and silent wisdom; good fortune comes of patient anticipation

Pajamas—emotional vulnerability and concern about making a fool of yourself

Panda—a need for privacy or confidentiality in a family situation

Pelican—parental devotion

Penguin—do not boast of your accomplishments or fly beyond your power

Picnic—a wish that some part of your life be more relaxed and informal than convention has allowed

Pine tree—long life, celebration, and joy

Pond—a period of calm reflection

Racetrack—exhilarating uncertainty and enjoyable risks

159

Sea—powerful unfulfilled needs; waves remind you that the momentum you need to realize your desires comes from trusting your own instincts

Seal—you are blaming yourself for failing to reach an impossible goal

Shells—extravagance and advancement at the expense of others

Shoes (dirty)— think before you speak or your bluntness may cause offense!

Shoes (new)—positive change and travel adventures

Silver—curb your spending; it may indicate over-reliance on a source of income that you should not take for granted.

Skeleton—dead relationships

Skiing—a project that is gaining momentum requires your immediate attention

Smoke—someone is trying to warn you about possible danger ahead

Snail—a need to retreat to safety in order to rediscover your inner light

Spider—you are feeling ousted

Spring—youthful optimism and the birth of new ideas, as well as cheerful companionship

Summer—prosperity and fruitful relationships, as well as cosmic intelligence and justice

Sun—aspirations: you will prosper in business and gain much needed insight

Sunflower—loyalty and longevity

Swan—prosperous outlooks and fruitful experiences, as well as the blindness of love

Tattoo—others are judging you superficially; believe in yourself and you will soon overcome unfounded criticism

Tea—if you are brewing tea, future indiscretions will make you sorry; if you spill tea you may suffer domestic uncertainty and tension

Teacher—inner guide with useful advice

Throne—craving power

Tree—a need for spirituality or the serenity arising from putting someone else's needs before your own.

Twins—aspects of your personality must be reconciled before you can form a union with like-minded people

Umbrella—preparation is better than prevention

Undressing—desire to be admired

Vampire—lack of energy

Veil—lack of honesty with your partner

Vineyard—balance between hard work and accepting the influence of forces beyond your control

Volcano—powerful outbursts

Visitor—good news

Walking—determination

Water (clear)—good luck

Water (muddy)—bad luck

Waterfall—vitality and a feeling of renewal will help you view the world from a new perspective

Weapons—aggression

Wedding—good news

Willow tree—anticipation of a sad journey during which you will enjoy the comfort and support of close friends

Windows—bright hope

Winter—material and spiritual gains after a period of rest and recuperation

Wolf—fierce independence and a predatory search for self-fulfillment; you may also experience a misunderstanding through your desire for solitude

Youth—temptation to live in the past

Zebra—be sure to focus your energy in one direction

Make a Dream Journal

A dream journal can help you overcome daily problems large and small, and decide on better ways to cope in the future. It could change your life.

Five minutes after your dream ends, you forget half the content. After ten minutes, you lose 90 percent. So keep a simple notepad, a light, and a pen at your bedside and record your dream immediately. If it is easier, dictate your dreams into a tape recorder or tell a friend immediately.

Transfer your dreams into a journal later. Over time, you will see the pattern of your subconscious concerns emerge.

Have you ever thought about writing a novel? Dreams are such liberating forays into the imagination that the practice of keeping a dream journal could be a great way to get innovative and unexpected ideas for a story.

Your journal can be a simple exercise book or a velvet-covered Book of Your Inner Self, locked so your secrets stay safe. For the front inside, ask a friend to take a picture of you in bed asleep, if you dare!

Consider noting any concerns or situations in your waking life. Are there any parallels in your dream? Consult the dream interpretations on pp.156-161 to analyze your thoughts.

Use two pages for each dream you record.

On one page, note:

- **The date (when you awoke)**
- **Location: where were you in your dream?**
- **Colors**
- **Sounds**
- **Objects**
- **Characters**
- **Emotions**
- **Significant images**
- **How did you feel?**
- **Did those feelings change during the dream?**

Draw sketches if you want to, rather than writing.

The second page is for your waking self. Note any books or television programs you had been watching before sleep. Describe changes in your sleeping habits, too—were you away from home, sleeping in a different place? Had you eaten any particular food or had a special drink? Could the dream, if disturbing, be the product of something disturbing you had only just seen?

Nightmares

Nightmares are our unacknowledged fears coming to the surface. They can be quite traumatic, and in some cases, become recurrent. For some, unpleasant dreams or nightmares repeat in actual content. For others, the content may change while the theme remains the same: scenes of falling, being pursued, being naked in public, or being late for class or a presentation are particularly common. Many dream theories concur that this type of experience is associated with lack of progress by the dreamer to recognize and solve related conflicts in life.

Carl Jung, a Swiss-German psychoanalyst, observed that portions of our whole personality are frequently projected outward in dreams, taking the form of aggressors, devils, monsters, intimidating animals, or natural events such as tidal waves. Jung referred to these symbolic figures as "the shadow." Fear of nightmares from early in life and other anxieties can block dream recall, but this can usually be overcome by learning about the useful nature of dreams. In fact, many nightmares signal opportunities for healing and insight, and can warn of psychological imbalances that need to be remedied.

Post-traumatic stress nightmares (PSN) are the subconscious attempting to deal with real-life trauma.

Eating cheese or chocolate before bed can trigger vivid nightmares.

Night terrors can be caused by some medicines or trauma. A dream appears to "transfer" itself to the waking surroundings. The subject wakes, eyes open, glued to the bed with terror. Or a child sits up, looking at something invisible in the corner of the room. He or she ignores a parent's soothing voice, and may include them in the terror by screaming, "Go away!" or add them into the dream by saying, "Look…" He or she may ask for Mummy or Daddy, even if they're already there. The parent should put all the lights on to dispel the terrifying image or wake him or her gently with a warm flannel on the face.

Sleeping Beauty

Written by French author Charles Perrault in 1697 as part of his
Mother Goose Tales, this enduringly popular folk tale has been
immortalized by Tchaikovsky in his ballet of 1890, and by the Walt
Disney cartoon in 1959.

A baby princess has three fairy godmothers, who endow her with
desirable qualities at her baptism. The ceremony is interrupted by a
wicked fairy, who curses the princess. She commands that the princess
will prick her finger and die at age 16. The third good fairy commutes this
to sleep, rather than death.

At 16, the princess is enticed by the disguised bad fairy to prick
her finger on a spinning wheel. She falls asleep, with the court
around her. A hedge of thorns hides the castle.

A century later, a prince hacks through it and awakens the princess
with true love's kiss—the only antidote to the sleep spell. The court
awakes and rejoices at their marriage.

But there is a second part to Charles Perrault's story, which is little
known. The marriage is kept secret for two years. They have a daughter,
Aurora, and a son, Jour. When the Princess's mother-in-law, an ogress,
discovers this, she wants to eat them up, but is outwitted and dies.

The story can be enjoyed simply, it but also has connections with
fertility myths such as that of Persephone, the Greek Goddess of Spring,
who needs to be awakened by Winter with a kiss. The children's names,
Dawn and Day, point to origins as a prayer to the Sun.

Some psychologists interpret the story differently. At 16, the age of
sexual maturity, the princess falls asleep. Her full sexual awakening by a
prince heralds the beginning of a life of adult troubles, especially from her
mother-in-law!

EXTRACT FROM

Sleeping Beauty in the Woods

by

CHARLES PERRAULT

The prince made his way into a great courtyard, paved with
marble, and mounting the staircase entered the guardroom.
Here the guards were lined up on either side in two ranks,
their muskets on their shoulders, snoring their hardest.
Through several apartments crowded with ladies and
gentlemen in waiting, some seated, some standing, but all
asleep, he pushed on, and so came at last to a chamber
which was decked all over with gold. There he encountered
the most beautiful sight he had ever seen. Reclining upon a
bed, the curtains of which on every side were drawn back,
was a princess of seemingly some fifteen or sixteen summers,
whose radiant beauty had an almost unearthly luster.

Trembling in his admiration he drew near and went on
his knees beside her. At the same moment, the hour of
disenchantment having come, the princess awoke, and
bestowed upon him a look more tender than a first glance
might seem to warrant.

"Is it you, dear prince?" she said. "You have been long
in coming!"

Charmed by these words, and especially by the manner
in which they were said, the prince scarcely knew how to
express his delight and gratification. He declared that he
loved her better than he loved himself.

Guardian Angels

It may comfort children, the sick, or anyone with a heavy heart, to know that his or her guardian angel, a blessed heavenly spirit, is protecting them as they sleep.

Many people of all religions believe in guardian angels. They are said to protect their charges against evil and to give guidance. George Washington credited his success at Valley Forge to "an inspiring visit from a heavenly being." Abraham Lincoln constantly invoked the wisdom of angels to help him govern.

During World War I, in Mons, Belgium on August 23, 1914, thousands of soldiers reported seeing an angel hover above them on the battlefield. Their story of a heavenly savior soon turned into legend, and the angel was credited with casting a protective shadow over the British army.

You may find your personal guardian angel when you ask for help and are kind to others. Although children and the elderly report seeing winged figures, angels are rarely seen. But you may suddenly feel especially loved and hear a quiet voice in your head, saying: "Don't worry," or "Wait: things will turn out fine."

Through the long night-watches, May thine angels spread,
Their white wings above me, Watching my bed.

from *Now The Day Is Over*, Sabine Baring-Gould

Children's Dream Beds

Today, children have fantasy beds in the shapes of trains or castles to encourage them to enjoy bedtime. There are bedstyles to suit every budget, from snap-together plastic to made-to-order, carved heirlooms.

Most little girls would love to be driven to dreamland in a bed like Cinderella's coach, with a real door. Boys might want a race car or an old-fashioned train. The more imaginative the design of the bed, the more the child will look forward to going to bed at night! But remember that children grow up fast, and a new, less childish bed may soon be called for.

A desk in the bedroom might encourage children to do their homework in peace away from the family. But televisions and computers can tempt children to stay up too late.

Older children might want a twin-over-full bunk bed, which sleeps two on the base unit and a third friend on top. If you have bunk beds to save space, be sure to put the older child on top. It is also recommended that the child is more than six years old before sleeping on the top bunk.

Try not to give a child a bed that folds away during the day. Everyone needs a space they can call their own.

Hammocks As Beds

A hammock strung between two leafy trees is the epitome of relaxation in the outdoors. It has many happy and romantic associations, from the Mediterranean siesta to the castaway on a desert island. It truly does represent the easy life. Everyone is happy to idle away some time in the embrace of a hammock and be transported by the breeze, the hum of bees, and the perfume of the trees to their own desert island. And because they can be taken down, rolled up, and stored, they are great space-saving beds. More than 100 million people in Africa, China, the Philippines, and South America use hammocks daily.

Columbus' first sight in the New World was the natives of the Bahamas asleep in hammocks. He took some home, and soon the idea spread to every European navy. Stuffed into holes in ships, they repelled gunfire too.

Today, there are three main hammock styles. Mayan hammocks are woven from diamonds of thin cotton cord which provides comfortable "give" and stops you rolling out while sleeping. Mayan hammocks are considered very effective in relieving backache and reducing body tension. For those who prefer a solid sleeping base, the Brazilian hammock is made from woven cloth. Rope hammocks are the most sturdy, but are liable to dig into the back.

IN THE HAMMOCK

Make a Hammock

A hammock is easy to make—it is simply a length of wood with a dozen holes drilled into it at regular intervals and some sturdy rope threaded through grommets in a length of strong fabric—with the color and pattern to your own taste. To make the hammock clews, you can use either natural or synthetic strings. Natural strings are more attractive, softer, and easier to work with. Synthetic strings, on the other hand, are stronger and won't disintegrate when left outdoors.

Use the following instructions to make a new hammock or adapt or renovate an old one.

MATERIALS
- 3yd/3m of yellow and green canvas 54in/137cm wide
- 20yd/20m of $\frac{1}{2}$in/1.5cm-wide rope
- Wooden batten 1yd/1m long with 12 evenly spaced holes large enough to thread the rope through
- Two steel rings 2–3in/5–7.5cm in diameter
- 26 grommets
- Sewing kit

1 Square up the fabric. Turn in ¾in/2cm across the width for the top and bottom. Press. Turn in another 2in/5cm and press. Double topstitch in place.

2 Repeat step 1 for turning in the sides.

3 Find the center of the top and bottom seams and mark with a pin. This is the position of the center grommet.

4 Measure and mark with pins the position of six evenly spaced grommets to each side of the center pin (see figure A).

5 Insert the grommets following the manufacturer's instructions (see figures B-E).

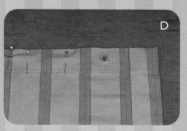

6 Thread a double thickness of rope through each side seam. Make a knotted loop at each end.

7 With a third length of rope, leaving a long thread end, begin at the left-hand side of the wooden batten and thread through the loop, then through the first hole at the left-hand side of the batten working from bottom to top.

8 Thread the rope through the steel ring above the center of the batten, and then back through the second hole in the batten (see figure F).

9 Thread the rope down through the first grommet (see figure G).

10 Thread through the next two grommets, up through the batten to the ring and back. Repeat (see figure H).

11 At the right-hand side thread the rope through the batten and knot the end around the loops at the end of the side seam. Repeat at the other end.

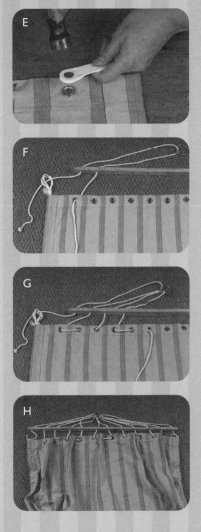

Come, cuddle
    your head on my
    shoulder, dear,

Your head like the
    golden-rod,

And we will go sailing
    away from here

To the beautiful land
    of Nod.

from *The Beautiful Land of Nod*, Ella Wheeler Wilcox

Heidi

by

JOHANNA SPYRI

[Heidi] found herself in the hayloft…

"I shall sleep up here, grandfather," she called down to him, "It's lovely, up here. Come up and see how lovely it is!"

"Oh, I know all about it," he called up in answer.

"I am getting the bed ready now," she called down again, as she went busily to and fro at her work, "but I shall want you to bring me up a sheet; you can't have a bed without a sheet, you want it to lie upon."

"All right," said the grandfather, and presently he went to the cupboard, and after rummaging about inside for a few minutes he drew out a long, coarse piece of stuff, which was all he had to do duty for a sheet. He carried it up to the loft, where he found Heidi had already made quite a nice bed. She had put an extra heap of hay at one end for a pillow, and had so arranged it that, when in bed, she would be able to see comfortably out through the round window.

"That is capital," said her grandfather; "now we must put on the sheet, but wait a moment first," and he went and fetched another large bundle of hay to make the bed thicker, so that the child should not feel the hard floor under her.

"There, now bring it here."

Heidi had got hold of the sheet, but it was almost too heavy for her to carry; this was a good thing, however, as the close thick stuff would prevent the sharp stalks of the hay running through and pricking her.

"We have forgotten something now, grandfather," she said after a short silence.

"What's that?" he asked.

"A coverlid; when you get into bed, you have to creep in between the sheets and the coverlid."

"Oh, that's the way, is it? But suppose I have not got a coverlid?" said the old man.

"Well, never mind, grandfather," said Heidi in a consoling tone of voice, "I can take some more hay to put over me," and she was turning quickly to fetch another armful from the heap, when her grandfather stopped her.

"Wait a moment," he said, and he climbed down the ladder again and went towards his bed. He returned to the loft with a large, thick sack, made of flax, which he threw down, exclaiming, "There, that is better than hay, is it not?" Heidi began tugging away at the sack with all her little might, in her efforts to get it smooth and straight, but her small hands were not fitted for so heavy a job. Her grandfather came to her assistance, and when they had got it tidily spread over the bed, it all looked so nice and warm and comfortable that Heidi stood gazing at it in delight.

"That is a splendid coverlid," she said, "and the bed looks lovely altogether! I wish it was night, so that I might get inside it at once."

Slumber Parties

These popular girls' overnight parties often prove to involve less slumber and more excited wakefulness, so as a parent, be prepared to hear squeals and giggles well into the night.

These parties are not gentle or quiet occasions. One young party-hostess confided that at her slumber parties, the first person who falls asleep risks an uncomfortable revenge: having their next day's underwear left in the freezer, wet, to wear the following morning.

IN

- **Personalized sleeping bags**

- **Pink pajamas**

- **Pizza**

- **Popcorn**

- **Painting each others' nails**

- **Playing games**

- **Photographing pals**

- **Pulling funny faces while brushing one's teeth**

- **Parents to pay**

- **Piles of clothes, discarded, for moms to identify whose is whose the next morning.**

OUT

- **Doing homework**
- **Talking quietly**
- **Putting the lights out**
- **Sleeping**

Lift a Gift
A SLUMBER PARTY GAME

Ask everyone to bring a secret, wrapped gift worth a specified sum. Guests should sit around the pile of gifts. Throw dice to decide who goes first.

The first player chooses a gift and unwraps it. Each subsequent player also chooses a wrapped gift, but BEFORE UNWRAPPING IT may, instead, decide to "steal" any gift unwrapped by a previous player, which she likes the look of.

The owner of the desired gift must give it up when asked. In return, she takes the gift-lifter's rejected gift, still wrapped. (When she unwraps it, of course, everyone hopes it contains something the "thief" would have preferred.)

The same gift can be repeatedly "stolen" until the end. The first player then gets her pick of ALL the unwrapped gifts, to swap with her gift.

(Keep a few extra wrapped gifts in the background, for cases of serious discontent.)

"You should not be the first one to fall asleep at a slumber party."

KATIE, AGE 12

Make a Sleepy Bear Pajama Case

**Anything that encourages children to be tidy is a good
training tool and a help to Mom!**

Finished size $14\frac{3}{4}$ x 14in/37.5 x 35.6cm when closed

MATERIALS

- $\frac{1}{4}$yd/0.25m of cream cotton for the bear's pillow
- 5in/13cm of green check cotton for the bear's sheet
- $\frac{1}{2}$yd/0.5m of blue stripe cotton fabric for the bag
- $\frac{1}{2}$yd/0.5m lining
- $\frac{1}{4}$yd/0.25m of red fabric for binding
- Fabric scraps for the appliqué motifs
- 1yd x 14in/1m x 36cm of 2oz wadding
- Coton à broder embroidery thread
- Small ball of blue and white wool for the pom pom
- Two large decorative buttons
- $\frac{1}{4}$yd/0.25m square of fusible web
- 14 x 12in/36 x 30cm of Stitch & Tear
- Small amount of Velcro to fasten

CUTTING OUT

1 Cut one length of cream fabric measuring $8\frac{1}{2}$ x $11\frac{1}{2}$in/21.6 x 29.2cm.

2 Cut the green check fabric to measure $3\frac{1}{2}$ x $11\frac{1}{2}$in/8.9 x 29.2cm.

3 Cut one length of blue stripe fabric to measure 2 x $11\frac{1}{2}$in/5 x 29.2cm.

4 Cut two lengths of blue stripe fabric 2 x 13in/5 x 33cm.

5 Cut one piece of blue stripe fabric for the back 17 x 14in/43.2 x 35.6cm.

6 For the lining, cut one front, 15 × 14in/38.1 × 35.6cm and one back 17 × 14in/43.2 × 35.6cm. Cut the same in wadding.

7 Cut two lengths of red fabric for the binding 1$\frac{1}{2}$in × 2$\frac{1}{2}$yds/3.8cm × 2.29m.

8 Trace the patterns provided to make templates for the bear appliqué motifs. Place the templates right-side up on the right side of the fabric and trace an outline. Cut out each shape.

9 Place the templates face down on the paper side of the fusible web and trace an outline. Cut out the shapes leaving a narrow seam allowance around the edges.

10 Bond the pieces to the fabric shapes with a hot iron.

MAKING UP

1 To make the bear panel, with right sides together, tack, then stitch the cream and the green check fabrics together along the length. Press the seam open.

2 Peel the paper from the back of the bear shapes and, using the picture as a guide, assemble the bear pieces. Place the wrist of the bear's paw just under the wrist of the nightshirt sleeve and the nightshirt neck edge just under the face. Place the inner ear just under the hat. Position the pointed hat piece last. With a hot iron, press the pieces in place. Once bonded to the background, the shapes will not come free, so

190

ensure that they are correctly positioned to begin with. Secure each shape to the background using slipstitch, blanket stitch, or a machine satin stitch.

3 Place Stitch & Tear under the cream and green background panel. With a wide satin stitch, appliqué around all the raw edges of the bear shapes.

4 Using three strands of embroidery thread, stem stitch and long stitch the features on the bear.

5 To make the pom pom, trace the template provided onto card and cut two. Place the cards on top of each other. Wind the white and blue wool around the cards until the hole in the center of the card is filled in with wool.

6 With sharp scissors and working at the outer edge of the card, cut the wool around the bound edge to reveal the two card edges. Pull the cards apart very slightly. With a length of wool bind the wool between the cards very tightly so that the short lengths of wool cannot escape. Roll the pom pom between your hands to make a good ball shape and trim any wispy edges away, leaving in place the two ends of the wool that bound the center.

7 Sew the pom pom onto the night cap with the wool ends and fasten securely.

8 To make the bag, place right sides together. Allowing a $\frac{1}{4}$in/0.6cm seam, tack, then stitch the bottom of the green front bear panel to a $2 \times 11\frac{1}{2}$in/5 × 29.3cm blue stripe length. Tidy the edges and press the seams open.

9 With right sides together and allowing $\frac{1}{4}$in/0.6cm seam, tack, then stitch the side borders to the bear panel. Tidy the edges and press the seams open.

10 Measure the bear panel and cut the wadding and lining $\frac{1}{2}$in/1.3cm larger all around.

11 With the panel right-side down, centre the wadding and then the lining fabric on top. Tack the three layers together.

12 Using cotton à broder, work a quilting stitch down both sides of the bear panel $\frac{1}{4}$in/0.6cm inside the raw edge. Trim away the excess wadding and lining to the same size as the front panel.

13 Place the blue stripe fabric for the back of the bag face down. Cover with a piece of wadding and a piece of lining cut to the same size. Tack around the outside edges.

14 To stitch the binding to the panel, with wrong side facing, fold a strip of red binding fabric in half along the length. Press in place. Turn under the raw edges $\frac{1}{4}$in/0.6cm towards the center foldline and press in place. Slide the binding over the edges of the panel and machine topstitch in place.

15 With wrong sides together, lay the bear panel on top of the back, aligning the bottom edges. Tack, then bind the bottom edge. Finish off securely. Bind the top edge of the back panel and the two sides, turning in the binding at the ends and finishing off securely.

16 Stitch two large, decorative buttons onto the flap at each side. For easy use for young children, stitch Velcro tabs to the inside flap to fasten.

These templates are at 50% actual size

The Tooth Fairy

There are many ancient superstitions surrounding teeth. If a child is born with a tooth already in his or her mouth it is considered a bad omen. There were many charms associated with teething, mostly to guard the child from evil during this period of change. The Vikings had a "tooth fee" which was given to children for the use of a tooth. The teeth were then worn as amulets. Until the end of the nineteenth century fallen and extracted teeth were saved until death and then buried with their owner. This included milk teeth, which the mother saved for her child because ancient custom decreed that the body must be buried complete. The dead must account for all their teeth or they will wander in search of them until Judgement Day. In other instances people would salt and burn the teeth so that others wouldn't be able to find them and work evil through them.

Today, when a child loses a baby tooth, he or she must place it under a pillow or sometimes in a special cushion clearly marked for the Tooth Fairy's attention.

Once asleep, the Tooth Fairy, a Celtic lass, takes the tooth and leaves a coin. She uses some teeth to build her magical ivory palace, and uses others to give her eternal youth or to boost her magical powers.

The fairy does not always come the first night that a tooth is left for her. Nor does she take every tooth, especially if the tooth has not been well cared for. Therefore it is vital to explain the importance of good brushing and dental hygiene to children.

She can be forgetful and leave the money with the tooth. Large teeth command a better price than small ones; but the going rate per tooth depends on the rise and fall of the world economy.

Make an Apple Pie Bed

This trick way of making the bed is traditionally played by children at boarding school or summer camp, but it can only be used on beds with sheets and blankets. It's often called "short sheeting" and is a cheeky trick children love playing.

The bed looks normal. But when the sleeper tries to stretch out, a mysterious blockage halfway down will bring their knees up to their chin.

- **Use a strong sheet. Place it on the mattress as if it is a bottom sheet.**

- **Fold it in half across the middle of the bed, bringing the top of the sheet up toward the bedhead.**

- **Add a blanket and fold the sheet over it, making it look as if the bed has a lower and an upper sheet.**

- **Add eiderdowns, covers, and pillows.**

To discomfort a sleeper more, remove the slats from the bottom of a wooden bed so that the mattress falls through when they get in.

Beds in the Middle Ages

The decline of the Roman Empire saw the decline in the luxury and opulence of the bed. People would "make a bed" from sacks of straw and sleep often in family groups huddled around a fire.

In a castle in medieval times the lord and lady's chamber contained as its principal item of furniture, a large bed with a heavy wooden frame and springs made of interlaced ropes or strips of leather. The frame was covered with a feather mattress, sheets, quilts, fur coverlets, and pillows. Such beds could be dismantled and brought on trips to other manors. The bed bore linen hangings that pulled back in the daytime and closed at night to offer privacy as well as protection from drafts. Servants and the common people of the Middle Ages slept on a pallet or trundle bed, or on a bench.

The Renaissance restored interest in furniture design. Artists, architects, and artisans drew inspiration from history and adapted classical designs. The bed became important and luxurious. Mattresses were made of pea shucks or straw, sometimes feathers, stuffed into coarse ticks, then covered with sumptuous velvets, brocades, and silks.

In the sixteenth and seventeenth centuries, mattresses were generally stuffed with straw or down, placed on a latticework of rope. The expression "sleep tight" comes from the need for the ropes on these beds to be regularly tightened.

Bed Superstitions!

If you say to an irritable person, "You got out of bed the wrong way this morning," you are referring to a superstition thousands of years old. The belief is that you should get out of the bed on the same side as you got into it, or you will have bad luck.

- **Also, placing a bed aligned North-South will bring bad luck. So turn your bed toward the morning sun.**

- **When making the bed, don't stop what you're doing, or you will spend a sleepless night in it.**

- **Don't put a hat on a bed: it brings bad luck.**

- **Never hang your clothes on your bedroom doorknob: it's a traditional sign that someone has died.**

- **Right foot forward—even the cynical, world-weary Augustus Caesar would not put his left foot on the ground first when getting out of bed.**

- **Sprinkle thyme outside your bedroom window to see fairies at dawn.**

Bed Sizes

Buying the right bed is a crucial and very personal choice, as Goldilocks discovered…

Not sure what bed size you need? Manufacturers can vary but here is a general guide to the different sizes available.

US/Canada

TWIN/SINGLE . . . . 39 × 75in/98 × 187.5cm

DOUBLE . . . . 54 × 75in/135 × 187.5cm

QUEEN . . . . 60 × 80in/150 × 200cm

OLYMPIC QUEEN . . . . 66 × 80in/165 × 200cm

CALIFORNIA QUEEN . . . . 60 × 84in/150 × 210cm

KING . . . . 76 × 80in/190 × 200cm

CALIFORNIA KING . . . . 72 × 84in/180 × 210cm

Europe

TWIN/SINGLE .... 36 × 75in/90 × 187.5cm

DOUBLE .... 54 × 75in/135 × 187.5cm

KING ....   60 × 78in/150 × 195cm

SUPER KING .... 72 × 78in/180 × 195cm

Asia/Thailand

TWIN/SINGLE .... 42 × 78 × 22in/
                             105 × 195 × 55cm

DOUBLE .... 48 × 78 × 22in/
                             120 × 195 × 55cm

KING .... 72 × 78 × 22in/
                             180 × 195 × 55cm

Goldilocks and the Three Bears

by

THE BROTHERS GRIMM

Then Goldilocks went upstairs into the bed-chamber in which the three bears slept. And first she lay down upon the bed of the great huge bear; but that was too high at the head for her. And next she lay down upon the bed of the middle-sized Bear, and that was too high at the foot for her. And then she lay down upon the bed of the little small wee bear; and that was neither too high at the head nor at the foot, but just right. So she covered herself up comfortably, and lay there till she fell fast asleep.

By this time the three bears thought their porridge would be cool enough; so they came home to breakfast…

The three bears thought it necessary that they should make further search; so they went upstairs into their bed-chamber. Now Goldilocks had pulled the pillow of the great huge bear out of its place.

"Somebody has been lying in my bed!" said the great huge bear, in his great, rough, gruff voice.

Bed Testing

- **Do you wake up with back or neck pains?**
- **Can you feel bumps, springs, or ridges under the mattress?**
- **Does your bed creak or crunch?**
- **Do you roll toward your partner in the night?**
- **Is your mattress more than ten years old?**

If you answered "yes" to any of these questions, your bed could be losing you an hour's sleep a night. Time to buy a new one.

Never choose a bed because you like the cover, or ticking as it's known. Try several beds in-store for at least five minutes, using this test for comfort and support:

Sit on the edge of the bed. Do you feel supported? If so, lie down. Slide the flat of your hand into the hollow of your back. If it slides in easily or your hips and shoulders feel uncomfortable, the bed is too firm and will reduce your blood circulation, causing tossing and turning when you sleep. If it is hard to slide in, and your body is sinking into the bed, it is too soft and will leave your spine tired.

If you have a bad back, don't automatically choose the firmest or "orthopedic" mattress. There is no medical standard bed. A survey by the Majorca-based Kovacs Foundation concluded that "medium firm" beds may benefit sufferers twice as much as very firm beds.

If each partner has different needs, look for mattresses that will zip together. Or it is easy to have a double mattress made in two degrees of firmness.

Before buying a mattress, check that it is suitable for your bed base, especially if it is slatted. And remember that when you buy a new mattress, regular turning is critical. Many experts recommend rotating your new mattress once a month for three months, and every 90 days thereafter.

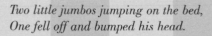

Two little jumbos jumping on the bed,
One fell off and bumped his head.

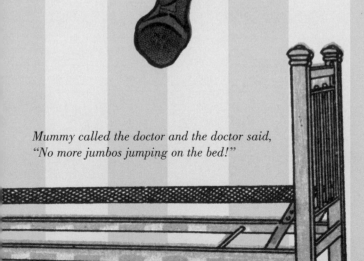

Mummy called the doctor and the doctor said,
"No more jumbos jumping on the bed!"

Finding the Right Bed

When buying a new bed, the basic things to look for are the width and length, and the type of base and mattress.

A bed should be as wide as possible and 4–6 inches longer than the occupant, as you increase in height by approximately half an inch during sleep, due to the rehydration of your spinal disks.

The base of your bed will depend upon the degree of firmness you require in a bed:

- **Boxspring/Divan** Based on ancient Turkish designs, a boxspring is a fully-sprung platform and looks like two mattresses in one.

- **Bed frame or surround** This is normally a bedstead design.

- **Antique beds** These will offer a firmer sleeping platform; old French or Scandinavian sleighbeds, for instance, probably have a wooden base. Remember to air these regularly.

- **Slatted bases** If self-assembling, remember to slot the slats into the holders so that they curve upward rather than downward.

Perhaps the most important component of the bed is the mattress, which should feel comfortable and mold to the shape of your body. A feather bed is the best remedy after a long, stressful day. Indulge in comfortable covers and a fluffy comforter. Down is a good choice for bedcovers, but synthetic alternatives launder more easily and reduce allergic reactions. Down and feather pillows are pricey but comfortable and, generally, last longer than synthetic ones. Side sleepers benefit from a firm foam pillow. Back sleepers are better off with a flatter pillow or one filled with soft down.

<u>OTHER</u> FACTORS TO CONSIDER:

- **Four-posters or canopied beds** can make a room seem smaller.

- **If space is tight,** look for a bed with a wooden platform around the edge, saving the need for a bedside table.

- **If you get hot in bed,** check out beds with micro-climate control covers. Allergy-sufferers will prefer antifungal or anti-dustmite treated beds, or beds covered with nonchemically-treated fabrics.

- **Choose a bed** that you can get through your front door and upstairs. Or one that unscrews. And don't wait till bedtime to put it together!

"Always buy a good bed and a good pair of shoes. If you're not in one, you're in the other."

GLORIA HUNNIFORD

Snow White

by

THE BROTHERS GRIMM

Then, as [Snow White] was so tired, she lay down on one of the little beds, but none of them suited her; one was too long, another too short; but at last she found the seventh one was just right, and so she stayed in it, said her prayers, and went to sleep.

When it was quite dark the owners of the cottage came back.…

The first said, "Who has been sitting in my chair?"

The second, "Who has been eating off my plate?"

The third, "Who has been taking some of my bread?"

The fourth, "Who has been eating my fruit?"

The fifth, "Who has been cutting with my knife?"

The seventh, "Who has been drinking out of my mug?"

Then the first looked round and saw that there was a little hole in his bed, and he said:

"Who has been getting into my bed?" The others came up and each called out:

"Somebody has been lying in my bed too." But the seventh, when he looked at his bed, saw little Snow White, who was lying asleep there. And he called the others, who came running up, and they cried out with wonder, and brought their seven little candles and let the light fall on little Snow White.

The Well-Tempered Mattress

- You get support from the mattress's inner springs or filling and comfort from its soft, breathable padding. People spend up to $20,000 on handmade lambswool, cashmere, and silk mattresses.

- **The cheapest open-coil mattresses have interlinked springs to spread weight evenly across the mattress. Look for at least 300 coils in a standard double to ensure optimum comfort.**

- Pocket-sprung mattresses often house up to 3,000 independent springs providing luxurious customized body support.

- **Latex mattresses provide support and ventilation, particularly for asthma- and eczema-sufferers as dustmites hate them.**

- Visco-elastic temperature-sensitive mattresses soften around your body so you don't feel pressure points.

- **Polyurethane foams can be supportive and hygienic and need not be turned regularly.**

- Air systems have springs or foam with an air layer inside, which can be adjusted for firmness at the flick of a switch by each sleeper as often as they choose.

- **Japanese futon mattresses are soft, thick unsprung layers of cotton. They need regular plumping.**

The Princess and the Pea

by

HANS CHRISTIAN ANDERSEN

There was once a prince, and he wanted a princess, but then she must be a real Princess. He traveled right around the world to find one, but there was always something wrong. There were plenty of princesses, but whether they were real princesses he had great difficulty in discovering; there was always something which was not quite right about them. So at last he had come home again, and he was very sad because he wanted a real princess so badly.

One evening there was a terrible storm; it thundered and lightninged and the rain poured down in torrents; indeed it was a fearful night.

In the middle of the storm somebody knocked at the town

LEFT: *The Princess and the Pea,*
by Edmund Dulac

gate, and the old King himself sent to open it.

It was a princess who stood outside, but she was in a terrible state from the rain and the storm. The water streamed out of her hair and her clothes; it ran in at the top of her shoes and out at the heel, but she said that she was a real princess.

"Well we shall soon see if that is true," thought the old Queen, but she said nothing. She went into the bedroom, took all the bed clothes off and laid a pea on the bedstead: then she took twenty mattresses and piled them on top of the pea, and then twenty feather beds on top of the mattresses. This was where the princess was to sleep that night. In the morning they asked her how she slept.

"Oh terribly bad!" said the princess. "I have hardly closed my eyes the whole night! Heaven knows what was in the bed. I seemed to be lying upon some hard thing, and my whole body is black and blue this morning. It is terrible!"

They saw at once that she must be a real princess when she had felt the pea through twenty mattresses and twenty feather beds. Nobody but a real princess could have such a delicate skin.

So the prince took her to be his wife, for now he was sure that he had found a real princess, and the pea was put into the Museum, where it may still be seen if no one has stolen it.

Inner Springs

One of the amenities of life enjoyed by the Arabs in the Middle Ages was sleeping on cushions thrown on the floor. This kind of sleeping surface was adopted by the Europeans during the Crusades. A mattress gradually became the padded foundation of a bed, formed of canvas or other stout material stuffed with wool, hair, feathers, or straw; in the last case it is properly known as a palliasse, or pallet. Modern mattresses can

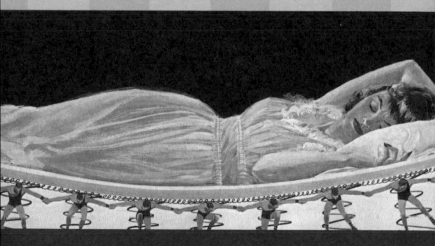

"INSTEAD OF A MATTRESS THAT LETS YOU DOWN...

last from ten to fifteen years, and modern technology has made sleeping in comfort possible for any budget. Just check the inside of your mattress. There are inner springs, foam, flotation and air systems. The choice is all about personal preference. The most conventional is the inner spring construction. Generally, the more coils a mattress has, the better the quality. Just be sure to compare coil counts within the same manufacturer product line.

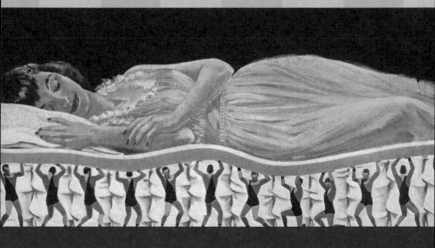

...GET THE BEAUTYREST FIRMNESS THAT LIFTS YOU UP"

Don't Let the Bedbugs Bite!

Granny's traditional bedtime salutation above refers to the little brown bloodsuckers who shared human beds for thousands of years. Exterminated in the 1940s by pesticides like DDT, they are returning to America and Europe in the suitcases of long-haul travelers.

Clean or dirty, bedbugs will live in any bed, as long as they can call a human "home." Their bites may not itch and are not infectious, and they resist modern pesticides. So if you notice tiny brown spots on your sheets and a sweet, sickly smell, call an expert. You may have to burn the bed to get rid of the eggs.

Fleas can also live in beds. If infested, spray or dose the victim with remedies from the doctor or vet, and buy a flea spray or "fogger," which fills each room with a slow-release spray. Fleas are hard to squash but can be drowned.

Finally, most beds contain about a million microscopic dust mites, eating skin flakes left in bed by your body. They can't harm you directly, but their minute droppings, when inhaled, cause asthma and eczema.

Controlling Dustmites

- **Buy mite-resistant synthetic bedding. Latex mattresses are ideal. Replace feather-cushioned seating with foam.**

- **Frequently wash all sheets, quilts, and pillows, at 104°F/40°C or hotter, to kill mites.**

- **Put soft toys and baby blankets in the freezer for a few hours every week.**

- **Use an anti-dust mite spray monthly, then vacuum mattresses and padded headboards.**

- **Make your home a fabric-free zone. Replace carpets with wood or linoleum, curtains with wooden blinds, and throw out mats.**

In My Lady's Chamber

Before modern plumbing inventions, people simply tossed the contents of their chamber pots out of the windows and onto the street below, with the warning shout "Gardez l'eau" (literally "watch out for the water.") A fragment of this remains a part of the British vocabulary today in the use of the word "loo," which is slang for toilet.

The chamber pot has been around for thousands of years—there are Roman examples from the first century B.C. They were made in various materials, including earthenware, tin, lead, pewter, copper, silver, and even gold. Wealthy Ancient Romans had silver and gold pots, which were brought in at intervals during their banquets—the Roman poet Martial described diners who snapped their fingers to summon slaves so they could relieve themselves into chamber pots without leaving the table.

The chamber pot in the form we now recognize probably appeared in the fourteenth century, and was commonly made of metal. When the colonists sailed to the New World, they would have packed a chamber pot along with other essential crockery items and tinware.

Before modern plumbing and ensuite bathrooms, elegant nineteenth-century bedrooms had a bedside washstand or commode hiding the chamber pot. Trick drawers or doors disguised the whereabouts of the pot. Somewhere inside you would also find a fold-out step used to mount the pot. Decorative pots might bear humorous slogans like "For a kiss I'll pass you this" or pictures of birds, ships, or patriotic wishes. Pots had lids and were emptied morning and evening by the chambermaid.

Canopy Beds

How did canopy beds and four-posters come to be? While people love to speculate about this question, the answer is most probably there in the name itself. The word "canopy" is derived from the Greek for "mosquito," and so it seems most likely that these draped beds were designed to act as a barrier against flying insects. Other more humorous theorists claim canopy beds were invented when house pets that kept warm in the rafters of homes repeatedly fell out onto their masters' beds. A canopy was erected to prevent a free fall. Hence the expression "it's raining cats and dogs," which originates from this particular theory.

As an added bonus, the drapes provided warmth and insulation from drafts. In the early days of European castles, the lord and his family slept in their chambers along with their attendants for convenience and security. For the sake of warmth as well as privacy, the lord's bed was completely draped. During the Tudor period, bed construction improved significantly. It was then that the feather bed made an appearance, replacing the straw mattress. Elaborate four-poster beds with lavish drapes were the mode, and indeed they were so highly valued that they were given special mention in wills of the time.

The most famous example was William Shakespeare. In

1616, as he was dying, he added this coda to his will: "to my wife the second best bed." Was this a snub to Anne Hathaway, his wife of 34 years? New historical research points to an answer by referring to another will, made in 1581 by Anne's father, discussing the fate of "the two joyned-beds in my parlor." It is now thought that Anne borrowed a bed on her marriage, and that William willed it back to her so she could return it to the Hathaway family.

Originally, the bed drapes were hung from the ceiling, but over time, a frame was added to support a canopy, or "tester," from which the drapes hung.

Four-poster canopy beds used in China during the Ming period were typically draped with fabric around the outside of the frame, which suited the season. Pongee silk or thick cotton provided insulation during the cold winters; and gauze netting offered relief from annoying insects during the summer without diminishing the refreshingly cool evening breezes. Silk drapes for a lady's bed were often finely embroidered with decorative and auspicious patterns. Curtains were drawn back during the day with curtain hooks, and the cozy cubicle continued to be utilized for dining and socializing.

Nowadays, a four-poster bed may be grand and traditional, in heavy oak with luxurious drapes, or it can be the epitome of cool style, with light, floating muslin.

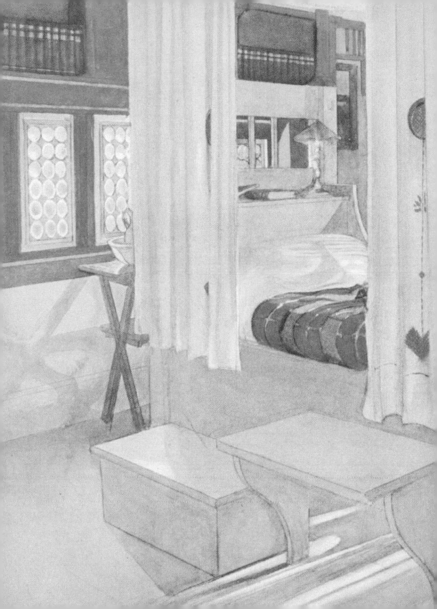

The Bedroom, by Carl Larsson

Weaves and Draperies, Classic and Modern

by

HELEN CHURCHILL HUNGERFORD CANDEE

The tendency of our day is to suppress the bed, to make of it a couch with the footboard abolished, or to obliterate its true character under innumerable silken cushions. To understand the pompous magnificence of the bed of earlier centuries one must realize the place it occupied in social— and even political—life, and it at once gains importance as an expression of other times and other manners.

Baldaquins, canopies, testers, all tell a tale, and curtains speak of display as well as comfort. In the time of Francis I it was a courtesy for a gentleman to put his bed at the service of a guest, actually to take him in as a bed-fellow. It must have been a severe strain on courtesy to take a formal sleep beside a snoring prince or nightmarish noble. Yet one hears that Francis I thus favored Charles IX, and the Duc de Guise the great Conde. Other customs there were equally demanding and all of them together give reason for the draperies which we use today in bed-rooms of sufficient size. Oddly enough the principal bed in the house served as a reception room. While still between the sheets of slumber's hours the man or woman of importance admitted persons who came on business or on friendship's quest.

Silk-covered extra pillows were provided for the recliner to place beneath the elbow, that guests might be greeted or papers signed with greater ease.

It was etiquette in the time of Louis XIV and earlier thus to receive visits of State. But most amusing was the custom prevailing among women of higher rank. On the loss of her husband the widow spent three weeks in bed in order to receive in appropriate setting the ensuing visits of condolence.

Catherine de' Medici, always interesting and intriguing because of the times she reflected, presents a magnificent picture of the luxury of woe. On the death of Henri II she tore down the gorgeous brocades of the bed and replaced them with more of magnificence than even color could express. Into this bed they popped the widowed queen, and this is how it was draped. A canopy was over her head of black silk damask lined with white. From this depended a dossier which hung behind the bed's head, also of black damask, but embroidered in silver. But the fine effect was given by the curtains long and full, all of black velvet. They were embroidered with gold and silver and finished across the hem with silver fringe. When they parted it was to reveal the queen lying under a coverlid of black velvet and black damask set off with flashes of silver and pearls. Who could doubt the sincerity of woe thus beautifully expressed? This style of bed was aptly called the lit de parade. ☞

Yet again, Francis I the elegant and artistic father-in-law of Catherine when wishing to curry favor with Henry VIII of England took with him a gift of a "camp-bed" in crimson velvet lavishly embroidered with fruit worked in real pearls.

The flight of Mary of Scots to England is one of the historic events which always stirs us. She was widowed, beautiful, and, oh, so young for the part she played. But she took with her thirty beds to soften the bleakness of her Scottish castle. Velvet ones were in the mossy green of summer woods, and they were also draped in crimson and in brown. There were damask ones as well, and satin, and these displayed shades of red, of blue, of yellow, and some were of white made lovelier by gold embroidery. All of them were rich with trimmings of metal and of silk.

It would appear that great ladies changed the hangings of

the bed as capriciously or as reasonably as they changed their gowns. We are told that they were sometimes short of stockings, especially those of silk, but never short of drapings for the vanities of the bed-chamber. Thus it came that the decorator and upholsterer grew ever more important, and the skilled sculptor in wood was without a bed to carve. Beds were so concealed by draperies that it was no longer reasonable to spend time and money carving them as they were carved in the days of Italy's High Renaissance.

Later the large square canopy disappeared and with it the long curtains shrunk to a drapery over the bed's head.

It was not altogether because of the cold that beds were curtained; it was to give dignity and prominence to the most important piece of furniture in the house. It is the habit of today to speak with flippancy of all things, a charming and witty flippancy. Nevertheless we can appreciate the sentiment of older times. I find it hard to express in modern phrase the respect with which the bed was regarded when it was considered worthy of such elegant caparison as we have been considering. Generations of deep sentiment about birth and marriage and death had crystallized into reverence.

Thus it was the bed as a family altar, or as a king's subsidiary throne, that it was considered appropriate to dress with ultra magnificence, this dress to be changed for varying circumstance.

And when now we drape our beds after the olden manner, a haunting seriousness flits through the back of the mind.

Wallbeds

The folding bed was patented by William L. Murphy. Murphy was born in Columbia, California, in 1876, and moved to San Francisco at the turn of the century. He and his wife lived in one room, and because he wanted to entertain, he began experimenting with a folding bed, and applied for his first patent around 1900.

The Murphy Wall Bed Company of California was founded that year. In 1918 William Murphy invented the pivot bed, which pivoted on a doorjamb of a dressing closet, and then lowered into a sleeping position—some of which are still in use today.

During the 1920s and 1930s, the popularity of the Murphy Bed was at its peak. During and after World War II, production remained low because low-cost mortgages and large family homes were readily available.

As people in metropolitan areas move into studio apartments, wallbeds are a practical and comfortable solution to limited space. Homeowners are converting bedrooms to home offices or playrooms and incorporating the wallbed with entire wall systems for storage.

Today, wallbeds are not the comedy beds of Laurel and Hardy movies, in which the surprised sleeper suddenly flips up into the wall. The makers insist that this cannot happen. These days, you can fold them away, complete with bedclothes, using remote controls.

RIGHT: A wardrobe bedstead designed by William Fay in 1878. This space-saving idea conceals a fold-down bed in one half and a wash basin with a jug and mirror in the other.

FIG.1.

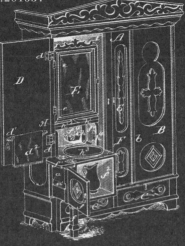

FIG.2.

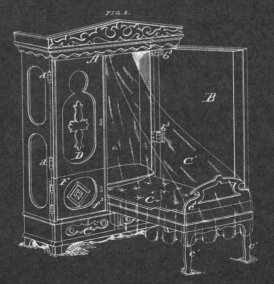

Japanese Sleeping Capsules

If they miss the last train home or don't want to stagger home drunk, Japanese businessmen have a cheap way of sleeping in the heart of big cities.

A "capsule hotel" offers fiberglass sleeping capsules, which are like futuristic space-pods for people, rather than rooms. In reception, you take off your shoes and place them in a locker. When you are allocated your capsule, you change in the changing area nearest it and place your day clothes in your personal locker there. Then, climb or crawl into your capsule. Some are "side-loading" while others are tubular and need to be entered at one end.

Capsules are not for the claustrophobic—they measure approximately 3 x 3 x 6ft/1 x 1 x 2m. But each has a radio, alarm clock, and television with a porthole or woven screen over the entrance for privacy. Capsule hotels don't usually take women or couples.

A California company is marketing a version suitable for people stuck at airports, so we may see more of these ingenious inventions in the near future.

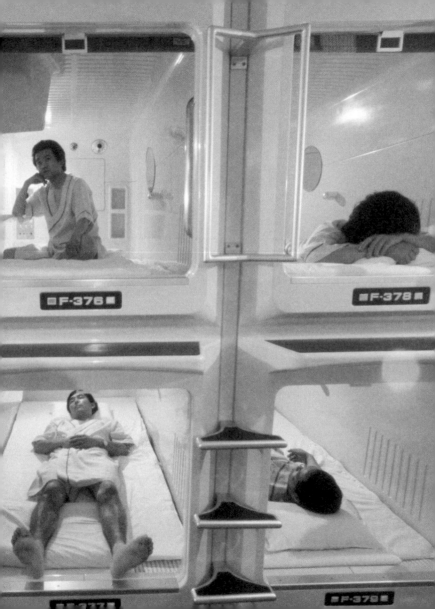

Power Napping

"You must sleep sometime between lunch and dinner, and no halfway measures. Take off your clothes and get into bed. That's what I always do. Don't think you will be doing less work because you sleep during the day. That's a foolish notion held by people who have no imagination. You will be able to accomplish more. You get two days in one—well, at least one and a half, I'm sure." Winston Churchill

They have known it for years in the Mediterranean, where siestas are an integral part of the day. Research at the Salk Institute, California, indicates that an afternoon nap has a similar effect to a full night's sleep to restore visual alertness, improve mood, and increase concentration. Scientists suggest that to get the best performance from staff, companies introduce office sleep bays and dormitories, one of which exists in Berlin.

Before the light bulb, people slept nine hours per night. The Washington-based National Sleep Foundation found last year that 61 percent of all Americans say that their decision-making suffers after a bad night's sleep; 37 percent say daytime drowsiness prevents them from doing their best work; and one in five workers outside the nine-to-five world—that's five million people—regularly fall asleep at work.

"Insomnia and sleep deprivation is costing American companies $18 billion a year in lost productivity," says Darrel Drobnich of the Sleep Institute. "I have a slogan: 'Be productive. Take a nap.' Companies are catching on. We're changing corporate culture."

New products are aiming at cashing in on corporate snoozers. The Company Store, a Wisconsin-based mail-order company, says business is great with its recently unveiled "Productivity Pillow," which includes a soft, European white goose-down pillow with pillow case, a snappy carrying case, and a treatise on napping. It comes in six designer colors, too.

Power-napping must be around 2 P.M. or 3 P.M.—the time when humans and animals experience a post-prandial dip or low ebb. 60–90 minutes is best for most people as deep dreaming sleep is most refreshing.

For the perfect power nap, find a dark space to lie down and use an eye mask, and ear plugs. If you're really pushed for time, a 20-minute nap in the afternoon actually provides more rest than sleeping an extra 20 minutes in the morning.

Simply closing your eyes and relaxing peacefully is refreshing in itself. Set a timer for 15–30 minutes, to allow you to enjoy the full rest period without looking at the clock.

Great power nappers include Margaret Thatcher, Winston Churchill, Ronald Reagan, John F. Kennedy, and Napoleon.

Pillow Talk

To make a bed inviting, don't skimp on pillows. Give each person two, plus an under-pillow, which is half the depth of a standard pillow, and extra little pillows for comfort, especially against an iron bedframe. Pregnant women, readers, and invalids will value a V-shaped pillow for sitting up against.

Pillowcases should be four inches longer than pillows. If you don't like antique lace, Oxford pillowcases with a deep border look best on top of a bed, and cheaper plain pillowcases can go beneath. Some people place top pillows in "pillow shams" or decorative covers matching the bedspreads. Remove these before sleeping on them.

Place pillows on top of the bedcovers, not beneath. Stack extra pillows in descending order of size on top of the regular pillows. Heap extra snuggling cushions invitingly at the end of the bed.

French double beds are traditionally made with a bolster or double-length pillow beneath the bottom sheet, with individual square pillows on top.

Notes should be safety-pinned to the pillow for the owner to see before getting in. Chocolates should be wrapped so they do not smudge. Gifts, apart from flowers, can be put beneath the pillow with the nightdress or pajamas.

Those who suffer from sleeplessness find comfort with hop pillows, and aromatherapy pillows for insomniacs or those suffering back pain or arthritis can be warmed in the microwave before adding their comforting fragrance to the bed.

A traditional Kenyan pillow is wooden, like a Japanese one, but with a small indentation for the head. You turn the pillow over to sit on during the day.

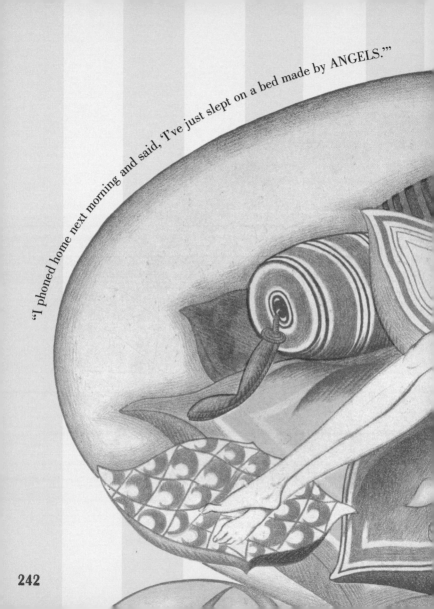

"I phoned home next morning and said, 'I've just slept on a bed made by ANGELS.'"

JULIE ANGOVE, of *One&Only Ocean Club, Paradise Island, Bahamas*

243

The Pillow Book

Sei Shonagon's "pillow book" is the sole surviving Heian-period example of what was probably a widespread practice among literate men and women. Japanese courtiers especially kept "pillow books" in the drawers of their wooden pillows to record their impressions and thoughts of the day before sleeping.

Sei Shonagon was a lady-in-waiting to the Empress Sadako around A.D.994 For five years, Sadako's apartments were the center of the court's cultural activity. *Makura no soshi* ("pillow book") is made up of about 320 separate sections: reminiscences, opinions and imaginative sketches, and lists, some with comments, others merely lists of words. It is a unique survival of this sophisticated court, with notes on the splendid silk costumes, complex etiquette, and even the weather— "snow is beautiful, except on the roof of a poor person!"

The last entry describes her mortification when another courtier found her book and made it public. However, the diary of her great contemporary, Murasaki Shikibu, comments that Sei Shonagon scattered her writings about the court herself with a self-satisfied air, and no good would come of such showing-off. But Sei Shonagon disappears into the mists of the past: we have no details of her life after 1001. It appears that she began *Makura no soshi* at court and finished it after Sadako's death, perhaps as late as 1010, and possibly presented it as a gift for Sadako's daughter.

Murasaki Shikibu was a courtier like Sei Shonagon, who wrote a similar pillow book, entitled *The Tale of Genji*. The two women were in fact members of rival literary circles. Murasaki was clearly aware of Shonagon's writing, and may have seen drafts of *The Pillow Book*. Murasaki voiced her opinion of her rival's character and writing scathingly in her personal diary. It is generally agreed that Shonagon was a witty conversationalist and Murasaki a reticent observer.

LEFT: *Murasaki Shikibu*, by Korin

"...When we got home Mother went up-stairs first and was met by Archie and Quentin, each loaded with pillows and whispering not to let me know that they were in ambush; then as I marched up to the top they assailed me with

shrieks and chuckles of delight and
then the pillow fight raged up and down the hall."

Letter from Theodore Roosevelt to his son Kermit, 19 October 1903

Pillow and Duvet Fillings

- Choose Hungarian goosedown for babyfine softness. More down filling than quill feathers gives a softer feel. Make sure feather pillows are pre-treated against smell and the fabric covers are tightly woven, preferably in old-fashioned Bohemian ticking.

- **Asthmatics can buy boilable feather pillows, or down mixed with white milkweed floss, but might prefer synthetics that can be boiled at 60°F/16°C, or for luxury, silk, wool, or cashmere.**

- The warmth of duvets is rated in togs, from 4.5 for a cool quilt to 13.5 for warm, and in the US, it is measured by "fill power," from 575 to 800. The higher the number, the better the quality and warmth.

- **You can buy quilts in button-together layers to suit the weather, or one quilt with a hot and cold zone, to suit partners with different temperature needs.**

- Duvets should have quilted or closed construction to keep the filling evenly distributed. Higher-quality duvets use a construction called "baffling."

- **Invest in covers for expensive pillows and duvets. They protect them from stains and dust mites.**

249

Alarm Clocks

Levi Hutchins of Concorde, New Hampshire, invented the alarm clock in 1787, though his clock could only ring at 4 A.M. But ever since Seth Thomas improved upon the design by inventing a mechanical wind-up alarm clock, people have been rolling out of bed on time. Grudgingly.

Indeed, an annual survey by the Massachusetts Institute of Technology asked adults which invention they hated most, but couldn't live without. Twenty-five percent answered "the alarm clock." Only the cell phone was disliked more.

The best alarm clocks today automatically reset themselves in different time zones, after they have lost power, or when clocks go forward an hour as in Daylight Saving Time. Some alarms also incorporate automatic weekend overrides for when you want to sleep in. Other new designs are clever enough to indicate the morning's weather.

One of the best-selling alarm clocks is the low-tech Bunny Clock, which looks like a rabbit face. When it is time to get up, the rabbit's eyes open and its ears spring up. This gives children who can't yet tell the time the visual OK to wake up their parents. 👉

You can also buy clocks to send you to sleep rather than wake you up. These play sound effects like white noise, tropical rain, undersea sounds or trickling water (not recommended for those with weak bladders). Others play a beating-heart sound, designed to emulate the feelgood sound of our mother's body while we were in the womb. Baby "get to sleep" toys also incorporate this sound effect.

Perhaps the best way to sleep well is to have two clocks: one to send you to sleep and the other to wake you up. If being woken suddenly by an alarm makes you tired and irritable, a light clock gradually brightens half an hour before you wake. The idea is that you feel ready to get up. Or it might prolong the agony of knowing that you'll be getting up soon.

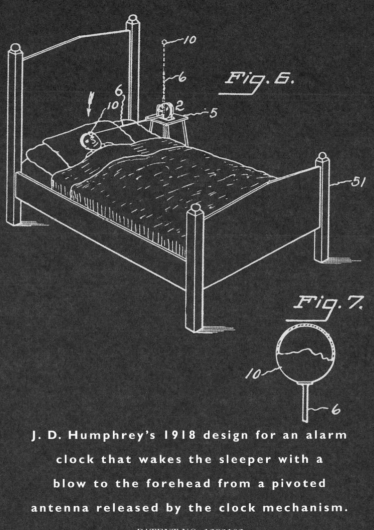

Fig. 6.

Fig. 7.

J. D. Humphrey's 1918 design for an alarm
clock that wakes the sleeper with a
blow to the forehead from a pivoted
antenna released by the clock mechanism.

PATENT NO. 1293102

The Sunne Rising

JOHN DONNE

Busie old foole, unruly Sunne,
Why dost thou thus,
Through windowes, and through curtaines call on us?
Must to thy motions lovers seasons run?
Sawcy pedantique wretch, goe chide
Late schoole boys, and sowre prentices,
Goe tell Court-huntmen, that the King will ride,
Call countrey ants to harvest offices;
Love, all alike, no season knowes, nor clyme,
Nor houres, dayes, months, which are the rags of time.

The Automatic Tea-Maker

The first tea-maker invented was probably named by an English gunsmith, Frank Clarke, in 1902. His creation was manufactured by the Automatic Water Boiler Company. It had a clockwork alarm, which tripped a lever drawing a sheet of emery paper past a match, striking it, and lighting the stove to heat the kettle. The kettle steam pushed another lever, which tilted the kettle to pour water into the pot. Or onto your pillow, if it went wrong.

Thirty years later the Goblin Teasmade was introduced by Hubert Booth, the inventor of the vacuum cleaner. It had an electric light, clock, and timers. Some bakelite art deco models sell for hundreds, and there is a flourishing market for spare parts and repairs to old machines.

In the mid '70s, more sophisticated models of the Goblin Teasmade featured inbuilt radios as a gentler way of waking up than an unpleasant buzzer. With every luxury, including a space for a family photo, modern tea-makers remain treasured bedside companions.

So if no one in your house is kind enough to offer to bring you a steaming cup of tea first thing in the morning, there is a simple, reliable solution!

Morning
Luxury

Up With the Rooster?

If you wake at 4 A.M. still sleepy, you may suffer from "early morning wakening," a common sleep disorder:

- **You might be going to bed too early. We need less sleep as we get older. Newborn babies need 16 to 20 hours; teenagers, around nine and a half hours; adults, around seven. At 80, we need an average of five hours' sleep, but can find it harder to stay awake all day.**

- Perhaps your bedroom is too light. Our bodies automatically wake up when light stimulates the brain. Use blackout blinds or an eyemask to get more shut-eye.

- Another cause of early-morning wakefulness is depression or anxiety. Sleeping pills will work for a time, but for permanent relief, you have to deal with the cause.

- If you wake with the dawn, taking sleeping tablets will make you feel groggy in the morning, biochemically your most productive time of the day.

Elsie Marley has grown so fine,

    She won't get up to serve the swine;

But lives in bed till eight or nine,

    And surely she does take her time.

Breakfast in Bed

There is no lazy Sunday treat like breakfast in bed, served on a butler's tray with two fold-out legs to give stability over the person's lap. To achieve a luxurious look, add a small vase of flowers, a white linen napkin and the newspaper. Another useful accessory is a small battery-operated table crumb hoover to clean the bed afterwards!

The classic breakfast in bed is a glass of Mimosa (champagne and orange juice), toast, scrambled eggs, smoked salmon, and caviar. Serve English breakfast tea in a pot with a tea cosy (like a quilted hat for the tea pot) or coffee with milk.

Eastern Europeans might prefer blinis and rye bread with hams, herring, pickles, cheese, and hard boiled eggs. Americans enjoy bacon, scrambled eggs, and pancakes with maple syrup, or if they are from the South, hominy grits, biscuits, bacon, and eggs.

A popular breakfast in bed at London's Savoy Hotel is actually Japanese. Served on a black lacquer tray, dishes contain miso soup (comprising fish stock, fermented soy paste, seaweed, bean curd, and vegetables), fish, marinated vegetables, an omelette, salmon, and rice, with green tea.

Braveheart's Breakfast

Scottish oatmeal is the perfect one-dish breakfast in bed. The oats contain high levels of soluble fiber to help lower your cholesterol and slowly release energy to keep you going.

For authentic porridge, use medium-ground oats rather than rolled oats, and serve in a wooden bowl with a horn spoon. Always stir clockwise.

To serve two:

- $2\frac{1}{2}$ cups/600ml water; $2\frac{1}{2}$ cups/600ml milk
- $2\frac{1}{2}$oz/$2\frac{1}{2}$ rounded tbsp medium-ground oats
- **Pinch of salt**

Bring the liquid to a rolling boil in a non-stick pan. Slowly pour the oatmeal in, stirring vigorously with a wooden spoon until it returns to a boil. Reduce the heat, cover, and simmer gently for 15 minutes, stirring gently. Add the salt. Simmer for five minutes, until it is thick but pourable.

Serve with a side bowl of cream, into which each spoonful is dipped before eating. Add sugar, a wee dram of whisky, jam or fruit. Then put on your trews (trousers) and wrap your naked torso in a tartan blanket, get up and go out into the driving rain.

Father, we thank
Thee for the night,
And for the pleasant
morning light,
For rest and food
and loving care,
And all that makes
the world so fair.

Help us to do the
things we should,
To be to others
kind and good,
In all we do,
in work and in play,
To grow more
loving everyday.

LEFT: *Suspense*, by Charles Burton Barber

The House of Mirth

by

EDITH WHARTON

As she entered her bedroom, with its softly-shaded lights, her lace dressing-gown lying across the silken bedspread, her little embroidered slippers before the fire, a vase of carnations filling the air with perfume and the last novels and magazines lying uncut on a table beside the reading-lamp, she had a vision of Miss Farish's cramped flat, with its cheap conveniences and hideous wall-papers. No; she was not made for mean and shabby surroundings, for the squalid compromises of poverty. Her whole being dilated in an atmosphere of luxury…

The next morning, on her breakfast-tray, Miss Bart found a note from her hostess.

'Dearest Lily,' it ran, 'if it is not too much of a bore to be down by ten, will you come to my sitting-room to help me with some tiresome things?'

Lily tossed aside the note and subsided on her pillows with a sigh. It was a bore to be down by ten—an hour regarded at Bellomont as vaguely synchronous with sunrise—and she knew too well the nature of the tiresome things in question. Miss Pragg, the secretary, had been called away, and there would be notes and dinner-cards to write, lost addresses to hunt up, and other social drudgery to perform. It was understood that Miss Bart should fill the gap in such emergencies, and she usually recognised the obligations without a murmur.

Today, however, it renewed the sense of servitude which the previous night's review of her cheque-book had produced. Everything in her surroundings ministered to feelings of ease and amenity. The windows stood open to the sparkling freshness of the September morning, and between the yellow boughs she caught a perspective of hedges and parterres leading by degrees of lessening formality to the free undulations of the park. Her maid had kindled a little fire on the hearth, and it contended cheerfully with the sunlight which slanted across the moss-green carpet and caressed the curved sides of an old marquetry desk. Near the bed stood a table holding a breakfast tray, with its harmonious porcelain and silver, a handful of violets in a slender glass, and the morning paper folded beneath her letters. There was nothing new to Lily in these tokens of a studied luxury; but, though they formed a part of her atmosphere, she never lost her sensitiveness to their charm...

Mrs Trenor's summons, however, suddenly recalled her state of dependence, and she rose and dressed in a mood of irritability that she was usually too prudent to indulge...

The matter-of-course tone of Mrs Trenor's greeting deepened her irritation. If one did drag one's self out of bed at such an hour, and come down fresh and radiant to the monotony of note-writing, some special recognition of the sacrifice seemed fitting.

"The next morning, on her breakfast tray, Miss Bart found a note from her hostess."

Guest Bedrooms

Make a guest bedroom inviting with a bottle of drinking water by the bed, freshly cut flowers, a basket of fruit, interesting books and magazines to read, toothpaste, new toothbrushes, fluffy white towels, and a face cloth.

Often other people's homes seem colder, so provide extra blankets. Check on whether your guest has any medical needs, and make sure asthmatics don't have feather duvets or pillows, and that those with eczema have cotton bedding washed in non-biological laundry powder.

When you're a guest, bring a gift, but preferably not flowers, which need the hostess' attention to arrange when she is busy settling you in and cooking a special meal.

If you are staying for any length of time, fit in with the family and go out by yourself when you can. Take your hosts out to dinner for the evening.

A good guest always handwrites a "thank you" note to arrive within a day of his departure.

"...one should always sleep in all of one's guest beds, to make sure that they are comfortable."
ELEANOR ROOSEVELT

An American Original

Not so long ago, most people had candlewick bedspreads in their homes. They were immensely popular, especially after they became a mass-produced, reasonably priced commodity. Candlewick bedcovers had many advantages; they were cozy because of their tufted texture, but not too heavy, as they were made of cotton; they were decorative because of their wide range of color and pattern; and they could be washed time after time—until their colors eventually faded into gentle pastel hues. They are now just a distant memory of childhood for many people—though some collectors regard them as retro icons.

These familiar household favorites are one of those quirky American inventions that themselves originated in colonial handicraft skills. The colonial settlers had already brought their knowledge of intricate embroidery patterns with them to their new homeland. Those who were unable to obtain desirable embroidery materials such as silks and fine linens had to rely upon their creative ingenuity: during the 1700s, many women used left-over bits of candlewick to make tufted outlines of the intricate patterns that they already knew and loved. This homespun craft (called candlewicking) was mainly based in the self-sufficient plantations of the American South, and thrived there until it went out of fashion after 1850.

Fortunately, the beautiful bedspreads that were created through these years were lovingly preserved. That's how 12-year-old Catherine Evans from Dalton, Georgia, was able to see an example that had been left to her cousin. Catherine was fascinated by the quilt, and, three years later, she had made her own version after working out how the original must have been created. Instead of using candlewicks, she simply spun a thicker yarn to act as an equivalent material.

Catherine made a candlewick bedspread as a wedding present for her sister-in-law; a neighbor admired it and placed an order; then other orders followed. The trend caught on, and before long, by 1910, Dalton became the center of a thriving cottage industry, with people working out of their homes producing these handcrafted spreads. They were displayed on washing lines running along Dalton's local Highway 41. These were called "Spreadlines," and the local women sold their hand-tufted spreads to tourists passing through. Hence the highway gained its various nicknames such as "Bedspread Boulevard" and "Peacock Alley" (the latter probably due to the "signature" peacock motif used for large numbers of spreads). Eventually, candlewick bedspreads were made on specialist tufting machines. However, the cottage industry in hand-tufted bedspreads continued to flourish even after mass manufacturing sent candlewick bedspreads into homes all over America and Europe.

"The perfection of inspired luxury in

candlewick's thick, finger-deep texture."

The Rise of Twin Beds

By the end of the 1920s, Hollywood was Sin City. Stories of stars' parties, promiscuity, drugs, and even murders appeared at an alarming rate. And films reflected the times—gangsters, the creation of new music genres such as jazz, illegal alcohol use, and gambling—Hollywood portrayed it all.

But after a series of screen actors were embroiled in high-profile scandals that intensified already incensed moral censors, studio heads decided to censor themselves. After several permutations and more pressure from outside forces, the Motion Picture Production Code was created, more popularly known as the Hays Code after its champion William Hays, the head of the Motion Picture Producers and

Distributors of America. There was a bevy of new rules filmmakers had to follow. Sex, drugs, and immorality were out, and wholesome entertainment was in.

Films could no longer hint that people had sex. Even married couples in films could not share a bed. Exit the double bed. Enter conjugal twin beds. If anyone did embrace on a bed, one person had to keep a foot on the floor.

This artificially-created film fashion boosted twin-bed sales for a time. Fortunately, in real life, newlyweds could see few advantages in twin beds and soon pushed them together.

The Hays code was abandoned in 1968 in favor of the current age-based film-rating system.

Make a Quilt

The Shakers wove blankets in check patterns, most often in blue, red or black on a white ground.

This Shaker-inspired quilt has an antique, puckered look because the cotton batting stitched inside the quilt is designed to shrink when the quilt is first washed. The quilt layers are stitched by machine along the patchwork seams. The batting bounces back on either side after stitching to create a ditch, and so this technique is known as "in the ditch" quilting. It is worked with quilter's invisible thread, which makes it look hand quilted.

The quilting of the large cream squares is completed by hand. The simple Shaker house motif that decorates these large squares is taken from one of the many maps that show the layout of the Shaker communities. These early maps were naively drawn without perspective—with some of the houses drawn upside down or even balanced on the roofs of others—but they still provide a precious lasting record of the Shaker way of life.

As a finishing touch, the quilt is bound with strips cut from a large check fabric in the same two colors as the patchwork fabric.

The nine-patch quilt is made from three different blocks, arranged to form a subtle diamond pattern. If you can't find the correct width of muslin at your fabric store, sew two narrower pieces together to make the backing.

Sewing machine skills required

MATERIALS
- $\frac{3}{4}$yd/0.75m and 1yd/1m of two small check homespun fabrics
- $\frac{1}{2}$yd/0.5m of a larger check homespun fabric
- $2\frac{3}{4}$yd/2.5m of 108in/2.75m-wide natural American muslin
- 60 x 85in/152 x 215cm cotton batting
- Rotary cutter, mat and quilting ruler
- Cream cotton thread
- Quilter's invisible thread
- Strong quilting thread
- Sewing machine and sewing kit
- Iron
- Paper and pencil

Finished size: about 57 × 79½in/145 × 202cm

1 Press the patchwork fabric with a steam iron to remove any creases. Fold and press the selvages together, matching the checks in both layers. Turn the folded edge up to the selvage edge and press. Make sure that the checks run parallel in each layer.

2 Allow the fabric to cool and then lift onto the cutting mat. Align the pressed fold with one marked line on the ruler. Hold the ruler firmly in place and cut off the uneven edge of the fabric (see figure A).

3 Work across the fabric, cutting 4½in/11.5cm wide strips. Open out the first strip to confirm that you are cutting straight and that the checks are aligned through the layers.

4 Turn the first strip until it is horizontal. Straighten the end in the same way as before. Cut 4½inin/11.5cm squares from the strip. Cut 48 squares in one small check and 85 squares in the other (see figure B).

5 Cut 128 4½in/11.5cm muslin squares. Use the 48 check squares and the muslin squares to speed-piece the first set of blocks. Sew a check and muslin square together with right sides facing. Use the side of the presser foot as a guide to make a ¼in/6mm seam (see figure C).

6 Without breaking the thread, feed the next two patches under the presser foot, the other way up, and then stitch the last pair in the same way as the first. This block has four check and five cream squares.

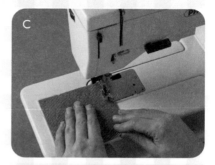

7 Add a cream square to the other side of the first pair, a check square to the middle row, and a cream square to the last row. You now have a block held together with thread ties. Make another 11 blocks the same (see figure D).

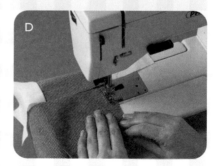

8 Snip the first block apart and press the seams in each row toward the dark fabric. Pin the rows together with right sides facing, matching the seam lines (see figure E).

9 Sew the rows together and press the seams into the center. Using the other small check fabric, make 17 blocks with five check squares and four cream squares. Press as before.

10 The blocks will be approximately $12\frac{1}{4}$in/31cm square. Cut 6 cream squares the same size. Begin to piece the blocks together. Pin a four-check block to a five-check block, matching the seams, and sew together (see figure F).

11 The first row has a four, five, four, five, four block pattern. Make three more rows like this. The second row has a five, cream, five, cream, five block pattern. Make two more rows like this. When the seven rows are complete, press the seams again. Then, starting with a four, five, four, five, four row and alternating the two patterns, join the rows to make the quilt.

12 Press the completed quilt top thoroughly from both sides. Measure the quilt top. Cut batting and a muslin backing to size. Lay the batting over the backing, then smooth the patchwork quilt on top. Start in the center and tack lines out to the edges through all layers.

13 Tack again around every second row of squares to hold the layers together securely. Fill the bobbin with cream cotton and thread the machine with invisible thread. Loosen the top tension slightly and stitch "in the ditch" between the squares (see figure G).

14 Roll the quilt under the head of the machine as you go. Do not stitch the large squares. Complete all the stitching in one direction and then turn the quilt to stitch the other sides of the squares.

Draw a large, simple template of a house. Transfer in pencil onto the large cream squares. Hand quilt along the lines using a strong quilting thread. Trim the batting and backing to the same size as the quilt top (see figure H).

15 Cut 2⅜in/6cm-wide strips, two the exact width of the quilt and two 1½in/4cm longer than the length. With right sides facing and ¼in/6mm seams, sew the binding to the short edges. Fold the binding over the raw edge, turn under a seam allowance and hem stitch on the wrong side. Repeat for the long sides, folding in the extra tabs at each end and oversewing the corners neatly. Wash in warm water to remove any pencil lines.

American Trade Blankets

The blanket has always been integral to Native-American life and the tradition of trade in the Southwest. When the Europeans arrived and the Westward expansion began, it was a natural progression for the Native Americans to barter silver jewelry and other valuable items in exchange for the commercially manufactured wool blankets the settlers brought with them. Blankets were associated with paying off debts, showing thanks, or indicating status. Blankets were used as shelter, as curtains, and most obviously, for warmth. Even today, blankets are part of many ritual celebrations, such as births, christenings, and marriages. Originally, the blankets were made from woven plant fibers, animal hides, and eventually from fabric woven by hand from wool or cotton.

The first trade blankets had solid colors and a few contrasting stripes. The thick, striped Hudson Bay Company blanket was made in England and was traded by European trappers to the Blackfeet and Northern Plains tribes. While the importance of quality wool blankets as trading commodities grew, American companies such as Racine Woolen Mills in Wisconsin, Buell in Missouri, Capps in Illinois, and the Oregan City Mill started to manufacture woolen trade blankets. While the Oregan City blankets bore relatively intricate designs, the Capps' were simpler. In 1896, Pendleton Woolen Mills in Oregon became the first mill founded specifically to produce trade blankets, and their high-quality and ever popular blankets meant that by the end of World War II, Pendleton were the only American woolen mill still in business. The first Pendleton blankets featured stripes, blocks, rectangles, or crosses. In 1901 the introduction of the Jacquard loom allowed more detailed zigzag designs to be created.

By the end of the nineteenth century, many Native Americans had set up trading posts for food, jewelry, clothes, and blankets. These people, thanks to their trading posts, became the ideal market for the English and American woolen mills, which catered their designs to these most appreciative customers. Some mills even sent designers out to live among the Native Americans in order to gauge the designs which appealed most to the different tribes across the US and Canada.

Throughout America, the name Pendleton has become synonymous with the "Indian-style" blankets used in recent history as jackets or lap robes in drafty automobiles, or draped over the backs of couches, or folded at the foot of the bed. Today, older trade blankets are highly sought after, and their style is being emulated in the form of coats, couches, and teddy bears.